L'Oréal Took My Home

Monica Waitzfelder

L'Oréal Took My Home

The Secrets behind a Theft

Translated from the French by Peter Bush

With a Preface by Serge Klarsfeld

ARCADIA BOOKS

Arcadia Books Ltd
15-16 Nassau Street
London W1W 7AB

www.arcadiabooks.co.uk

First published in the United Kingdom 2006
This B-format edition published in November 2007
Copyright © Hachette Littératures 2004
First published by Hachette as *L'Oréal a pris ma maison* in 2004
Translation © Peter Bush 2006

A catalogue record for this book is available from the British Library.

ISBN: 978-1-905147-54-0

Typeset in Bembo by Basement Press
Printed in Finland by WS Bookwell

Arcadia Books supports English PEN, the fellowship of writers who work together to promote literature and its understanding. English PEN upholds writers' freedoms in Britain and around the world, challenging political and cultural limits on free expression. To find out more, visit www.englishpen.org or contact English PEN, 6-8 Amwell Street, London EC1R 1UQ

Arcadia Books distributors are as follows:

in the UK and elsewhere in Europe:
Turnaround Publishers Services
Unit 3, Olympia Trading Estate
Coburg Road
London N22 6TZ

in the USA and Canada:
Independent Publishers Group
814 N. Franklin St.
Chicago, IL 60610

in Australia:
Tower Books
PO Box 213
Brookvale, NSW 2100

in New Zealand:
Addenda
Box 78224
Grey Lynn
Auckland

in South Africa:
Quartet Sales and Marketing
PO Box 1218
Northcliffe
Johannesburg 2115

Arcadia Books is the *Sunday Times* Small Publisher of the Year

Monica Waitzfelder, born in Rio de Janeiro, Brazil, in 1953, has lived in Paris since 1984. She has directed opera at the Paris National Opera, the Théâtre du Châtelet, and at other French an international venues. *L'Oréal Took My Home* was first published in France by Hachette Littératures.

Serge Klarsfeld is a world-famous lawyer and Nazi hunter: he and his wife Beate have been active in bringing Nazi and Vichy officials to trial for the crimes they committed (perhaps most notorious among them is Klaus Barbie, the 'Butcher of Lyons'). He is one of the foremost historians on the fate of the Jews in France during the Second World War, and has published a dozen books on the subject. Serge Klarsfeld is president of *Les fils et filles des déportes juifs de France* (Sons and Daughters of Deported Jews of France) and is a member of the Office of the Foundation of the Holocaust. He is the recipient of numerous awards and honours, including the Foundation of French Judaism Prize, the Raoul Wallenberg Prize and the Prix de la fondation de la mémoire. He was made an Officer of the Légion d'Honneur and of L'Ordre du Mérite and received an honorary doctorate from Union College, USA.

Peter Bush is the translator into English of, among others: Pedro Almodóvar, Juan Goytisolo (Bush was awarded the Instituto Cervantes Ramón Valle-Inclán Prize for his translation of *The Marx Family Saga*), Juan Carlos Onetti, Leonardo Padura and Luis Sepúlveda (his translation of *The Old Man Who Read Love Stories*, published by Arcadia, won the American Literary Translators Association Best Translation Award).

I dedicate this book to the Queirel family,
to all those in the Resistance,
to all those still brave enough to fight
against injustice.

Contents

Preface

When it comes to robberies and reparations, compensation, indemnification or restitution, the possible outcomes are many and varied. Although they lost not a single loved one in the Shoah, some victims may unearth paintings seized by the Nazis, get them unhooked from where they hang in museums and regain canvasses to the value of €250 million, while other may not even recover a quarter of the value of a much more modest belonging.

Many factors are at play in these situations, particularly persistence and chance. Persistence allows solid, well documented cases to be established, the climax of long researches begun in family archives and pursued in the public archives of one or several countries.

Chance enters the scene when, at the end of a long process, a judgement grants you the right to recover all or part of what belonged to you, or else when the legal entity or individual that has been benefiting for several decades from the initial theft decides that someone is within their rights to reclaim the property they are profiting from and agrees to return it or pay the proper price for it.

Edith Rosenfelder and her daughter have been persistent beyond the call of reason; but luck has not come their way: L'Oréal, their adversary, has not had the elegance to make an offer in order to put an end to litigation and, in the last resort, the legal system has not forced L'Oréal to return the Rosenfelder's building that was seized in 1938 in Karlsruhe by Hitler's Germany.

Edith Rosenfelder is now seventy-eight years old. She is the daughter of German Jews: Fritz and Kaethe. Her mother was deported from France to Auschwitz on September 7 1942; her father died of sorrow and deprivation in 1945. She left for Brazil at the age of seventeen and married there; her daughter Monica Waitzfelder has dedicated herself to this David-against-Goliath struggle represented by the attempt to recover the land where their fine family home once stood in Karlsruhe.

Fritz R. was the first to seek refuge in Paris in 1936 and signed a power of attorney on May 24 at the German Consulate authorizing a person he didn't even know in Germany to look after all his property and business. The document was signed under constraint, Fritz's wife and daughter being still in Germany and under threat from the Nazis. The next day, May 25, Fritz received as if miraculously a residence card from the Prefecture of Police. On January 20 1938, thanks to the powers of attorney signed by Fritz, the property of Fritz Rosenfelder and his brother Karl was transferred to the BGV insurance company. After this sale, Kaethe and his daughter could finally leave Germany and join Fritz in Paris. As soon as war began they were imprisoned as Germans and, after the fall of France, as foreign Jews. Kaethe perished, Fritz died; Edith survived. As for the building in Karlsruhe, it was resold in 1954 to a German subsidiary of L'Oréal, in spite of the proven continued existence of its owners who had been dispossessed by the greed and violence of the Nazis. In 1961 L'Oréal became the direct owner of the land.

In 2004 at the Supreme Court dealing with this case, the Deputy Director of Public Prosecutions who presided advised that the fact the robbery took place in France at the German Consulate in 1937 meant that neither the considerable time that had gone by, nor the fact the consequences were felt in Germany, should prevent the French legal system from ascertaining whether that criminal gain from stolen property was well-founded and who were the beneficiaries. In the end the Supreme Court unfortunately did not find this was so and refused to pursue enquiries relating to the extortion of the signature for the order of sale.

L'Oréal could have reached an amicable settlement as suggested by Monica Waitzfelder, who valiantly picked up the baton from her mother,

Edith. She carried out multiple searches in French and German archives and threw light on each phase in the persecution of her family and the way it was dispossessed of its wealth, discovering on the many detours in her search for justice black marks not only over those opposing their demands but also over Jews and non-Jews who placed obstacles in her way rather than help her.

L'Oréal's past should have led this giant company to develop greater understanding of Edith and Monica: Eugène Schueller, the creator of L'Oréal, was also one of the founders of La Cagoule, the extreme right wing movement which collaborated with the Nazis and, which, among other things, blew up six synagogues in Paris in October 1941. Jacques Corrèze who was responsible for L'Oréal's business activity in the United States was forced to resign in 1991 when I revealed that, as head of the collaborationist organisation, MSR, he had expelled Jews from their dwellings in 1941. As for André Bettencourt, the husband of L'Oréal's owner, Eugène Schueller's daughter, he began his brilliant political career in the foulest of ways by publishing dozens of articles between 1940 and 1942 in *La Terre française*, a prominent agricultural affairs newspaper created by the Germans. Several of these articles have an undeniably anti-Semitic character.

L'Oréal has refused to take on board the nature of its own history as well as the nature of the history of the Rosenfelder family. In spite of everything, that might have led to a moving reconciliation, to a gesture of fraternity and an end to confrontations based as much on ideology as cupidity! What might have been never was. Monica will perhaps still be forced to fight for a long time on several fronts in order to defend their House in Karlsruhe, which has become more than a virtual house and a financial issue: a genuine matter of principle.

Serge Klarsfeld

1
It All Began…

First of all, I thought it must be a joke.

'Hello, I would like to speak to Monica Waitzfelder.'

'Speaking.'

'I am calling from the Prime Minister's Office.'

I wanted to laugh. And he wanted to continue:

'You never sent back our questionnaire.'

'Oh, it's only about a questionnaire!'

In cheeky, humorous vein. And then I chanced my arm:

'That you, Manu?'

'It's the second time I've rung you from the Prime Minister's Office. We are setting up a commission to look into the stealing of Jewish property. I believe your grandparents were deported?'

Then I changed my tone of voice: 'I'm sorry. I thought a friend was having me on… My grandparents did indeed live in France and were deported. And what's this questionnaire you mentioned all about?'

'A questionnaire about the stealing of Jewish property. Did you receive one?'

'Yes, but it asked impossible things of me…'

'Such as?'

'Whether I possessed a whole stack of documentation. How on earth could I? Everybody who was deported died. And all their papers bit the dust with them. Excuse my language, but that questionnaire really riled me.'

Completely unfazed by my outburst, he went on: 'You don't have anything then?'

'If my mother got out, it's only because the person who came to rescue her ordered her not to put her shoes on, to save time; so, you can imagine, documents… All I've known since I was a child is that my grandparents were the owners of a large Victorian-style house in Karlsruhe. My mother showed me a photo. It's all she has.'

'Well, that's a good start. Perhaps your mother remembers other things?'

'It's very difficult to talk to her about all that. She's pulled down the curtain on that period of her life. When I was small, I could see it upset her, but she never said very much. She would just mention the house.'

'Try to speak to her. See what you can learn from her and try to obtain documentation on the house. Perhaps you should start there.'

'I've tried time and again to get documents… I've never managed to put my hands on any.'

'What do you mean? You've never managed to?'

'They refuse to give them to me, my mother has been asking for them for years and I've tried several times.'

Now, I thought my interlocutor sounded slightly doubtful: 'But this house did belong to you?'

'My mother said it did.'

'Well, they must supply you with all the documents. You know, things are changing now.'

'Perhaps…'

My interlocutor left me his details. I apologized again for the way I'd greeted him and asked a few questions about the measures the Prime Minister's Office was taking. I should call him back and provide him with more information, and in the long run even meet him.

This all took place mid-December 1999.

The house… From my early childhood, my mother had told me: 'L'Oréal took my home'. As a little girl I didn't really understand what that meant. The only thing L'Oréal meant to me was shampoo, and I didn't like it very much because it made my eyes smart.

Later on, I saw a photo of the house taken by my great-uncle at the end of the 1920s, a photo he subsequently gave to my mother. The only record we possessed of that period.

I should add that in Brazil, where I was born, history has more to do with carnival and football than the Second World War. Not that the latter was never mentioned: in the Jewish community – comprising mainly various escapees from the Shoah – which we saw on a daily basis and which became almost a substitute for the family, some people would tell their stories. But my mother never told hers. I heard it said that she had suffered too much and should be left in peace. From time to time she had 'fits' which my brother and I never understood: she would sometimes cry, or be shaken by an unspeakable fear, and she'd be left prostrate… We'd then go and seek refuge with our neighbours.

As a child, I realized my mother was one of those who had suffered most among this group of immigrants. And then there was the story of the stolen house, which kept returning like a leitmotif.

2

The Redheaded Witch

I was born in Rio de Janeiro. Apparently I was a very placid child, but one to be watched carefully because I was interested in everything going on around me and often almost fell out of my cradle or pushchair.

My first word was *Wasser*. I like water: the sea, the swimming pool, rivers…

At home, we spoke German because my parents expressed themselves poorly in Portuguese. My mother also spoke French, but my father didn't. Nonetheless, they enrolled me in an English school. There were children of every nationality: Japanese, French, Irish and Yugoslav…and every religion. We had lots of fun discovering one another's culture. We also learned music, painting and dance, but by my third year in primary school, I was still unable to read or write, so my parents decided to send my brother and me to a Brazilian school. In less than six months we could read and write and had adjusted to our new school.

From the age of four and three respectively, my brother and I took recorder and piano lessons. We had terrific teachers. They were Jewish concert artists who had had to flee Nazi Germany and now taught beginners in order to make ends meet. But we had no idea of any of that at the time. After our lessons, our two teachers would tell us to sit down and played us a beautiful concerto.

I also had dance lessons from the age of three. I loved dancing. I was a very shy child, and the movements allowed me to express myself without having to talk too much. I also read a lot, particularly French writers translated into Portuguese: the Countess of Ségur, Dumas, Valéry, Saint-Exupéry, and later on Stendhal, Zola, Maupassant, Gide, Sartre, Camus… I loved to read and would devour everything that fell into my hands. I also loved to study. As the atmosphere at home was very fraught, I think I sought refuge in my studies.

My father had a job that forced him to travel a lot: he would sometimes be away for three weeks, spend a week at home and then be off again.

The Jews in Rio helped each other a lot. There was a large number, especially Germans and Austrians. Some had fled persecution; others had escaped the camps. All were slightly lost in this country that was so different to their European culture. My mother was one of the few who had come from France. She had a French friend, also called Edith, but who was called Editinha. Unlike my mother's parents Editinha's weren't deported; her father committed suicide before they could take him away. The other day, in conversation, she told me she was quite astonished by the amount I'd found out, for my mother, although a close friend, had never told her anything, not even that her own mother had died in Auschwitz.

I have a confession to make: up to the age of ten I was afraid I was a witch. I should add that I am a redhead and that there can't be more than ten redheads in Rio. People used to stop us in the street and talk to my mother about the colour of my hair and that would really upset me: I had read in books how in the Middle Ages redheads were thought to be witches and were consequently burned. I think it was around this time that I had an inkling of knowledge about Nazism. However, I didn't read books or go to films dealing with the subject, perhaps as a self-defence mechanism.

Later on, I studied medicine and worked as an intern in a hospital. I discovered another universe and tried to understand and help people who were in pain. Nonetheless, I was always attracted by music and dance, options my family didn't consider to be real jobs. I finally abandoned medicine and decided on the arts, despite the lively arguments such a choice provoked among my nearest and dearest.

I then began to study to be an actress, while continuing with dance. I also took singing lessons. I got my professional card as an actress. I belonged to some prestigious companies of the time that fused dance and theatre, and all was well with my life. But I felt something was still missing.

I woke up one fine morning in Rio, in the pretty maisonette I was sharing in Botofago, my head abuzz with a single idea: I must go to Paris. Initially, it seemed strange that I should have been visited by such a wish: I didn't know anyone there, didn't speak French and didn't even remember seeing a film recently about this city or anything else that might have suggested it. In the end I could only laugh at the fact that such a preposterous idea had passed through my mind.

It had no basis in reason; I was at last leading a calm, settled life after a difficult separation (even though I was the one who had initiated the break), I'd got over my father's death in 1979 and was getting to grips with a new job I really liked. I had written a master's dissertation in philosophy with great panache, my artistic career was more secure, I'd joined a company that was much in vogue, and I also enjoyed a good circle of friends. Moreover, while Brazil might still be governed by a military dictatorship, we felt the end of the regime was nigh.

But nothing I did could chase this strange idea from my head. The weather or my daily routines certainly couldn't; on the contrary, it became such an obsession that my head was full of nothing else every morning when I woke up. I found it all extremely unsettling.

I then told myself the only way I could calm down would be to collect information about Paris. But even if the dictatorship were on its way out, it was still a constraining factor and made it very difficult to get proper information about anything happening abroad.

Nevertheless, I finally yielded to the persistence and power of desire: I *would* go to Paris. I'd never behaved this way before, but now desire had been transformed into necessity.

My mother and I had never agreed on anything at all. She continually criticized the choices I made, to the point that I was now inured to her attitude. Despite our stormy relationship, we spoke on the telephone every day, and I told her what I was planning by telephone.

'I think that's an excellent idea', she responded.

To my amazement, for the first time in a long, long time, I heard her voice express approval of one of my initiatives. She didn't even ask me how I reckoned I'd survive materially over there or what money I'd use to buy my ticket, nor did she use the language barrier as a counterargument. Not a single reproach.

Despite her encouragement, I used to temper my ardour by telling myself I'd give up my plans at the first obstacle to appear on my path. It was in such a state of mind that I went to the embassy to ask for a European passport: if I were refused, I would stay in Brazil. I obtained one within a week.

I had mentioned this sudden desire to go to Paris to my contemporary dance teacher. This woman was a real character, a great artist and was very sensitive to issues of human nature. She carefully considered each and every one of her words; no remark was ever superfluous. She was as supportive as my mother: 'I think it will do you good.'

And added: 'I've always thought of you as a producer...'

She said nothing else. Producing... That was something which had certainly never crossed my mind.

It was only from the moment things began to take shape that I began to question the reasons impelling me to leave: what would I do once I got there? My music theory teacher also encouraged me in vain – 'you think like a European, go for it' – I still didn't understand the meaning of the steps I was taking.

One day, as I was leaving a music class, my teacher asked me for help: 'A great Italian guitarist is in Rio to give a series of concerts. Can you help him get to know Rio?'

I drove over to pick the guitarist up, and after we'd made our introductions he asked if it would be all right for a friend of his to join us who happened to be in Rio.

'Of course,' I replied.

His friend was called Philippe and lived in...Paris. It wasn't difficult to show off Rio; it's a wonderful city, the weather is always good and, for someone familiar with it, is packed with interesting places to show people. On that pleasant day we spent together, I told Philippe of my plans, however ridiculous they may have seemed, to go and live in Paris. He offered to put me up until I decided to return. And he added that he would even come to meet me at the airport. All I had to do was ring him and let him know when I'd be arriving.

Right then, I still didn't know what exactly was motivating my desire to leave. It was only in the course of my stay in France that I realized I'd come to discover my roots. And gradually, history took over.

I signed up at the music conservatory as soon as I arrived in France. I soon began to attend courses in opera production. And some theatre studies in order to learn particular stage techniques. I worked with great producers, like Strehler, who taught me a lot. I started working for the Opéra National de Paris in 1991, as assistant producer on Roman Polanski's *The Tales of Hoffmann*. Since then I have worked with a number of producers on many, many productions. For the Opéra, but also the Théâtre du Châtelet, the Capitole in Toulouse, as well as abroad; in particular, I produced Bartók's *Bluebeard's Castle* at the National Opera in Rio.

3

A Deafening Silence

I arrived in Paris in August 1984. From the following year, as I was in Europe, I started investigating the house my mother talked about so much. I made contact with various people I thought might be of help but drew only blanks. For Jews who had survived the Shoah there existed a process for returning property called *Wiedergutmachung*. Now, whenever my mother had recourse to it, she could never get hold of any documentation, and her lawyers told her that her case was already closed. I didn't understand why my mother had never received any compensation as other people had. I then asked myself this question: had my grandparents in fact owned this house or were they simply tenants? By now it was impossible to speak to my mother about anything related to the Shoah; time had turned silence into a habit. It was my father who had told me the little that I knew.

After these first futile steps, I didn't labour the point. I had to integrate myself into French life, learn the language and earn a living. I had come knowing hardly anyone and it seemed more difficult to set up contacts than in Brazil. Nonetheless, I started to hassle the bureaucracies whenever I had an opportunity. But the new friends I confided in began to make fun of me; some even said I was inventing everything. So I became reticent on the subject.

I have a paternal uncle by marriage, and he lives in Basle, Switzerland. I took advantage of a visit of his to Karlsruhe in 1993 to ask him to go to the land registry and order a copy of the deeds the German authorities keep of the current and previous owners of properties. When he informed them of the address, he was told it didn't exist. My uncle was fobbed off by this laconic response. He enjoyed no more luck than we did.

My head buzzed with the words my mother had so often repeated about the home L'Oréal had stolen from her.

'Didn't you even ask for the address of L'Oréal?'

'If they told me they've never heard of that address, it's because it doesn't exist.'

I found this strange, to put it mildly: an address can be altered, the name of a street can be changed, but to do that and not inform the city land registry! I mentioned it to Angela who helped me write letters in German (although German is my mother tongue, I've never learned to write it). Angela was – and still is – my translator and, as she translated a series of documents for me, I watched her wax more and more indignant. She was also always extremely supportive. We then decided to write to the mayor of Karlsruhe to ask him for the new name of the street, explaining that my family had lived there and I wanted to pay the town a visit. His reply was long in coming but, in a helpful letter, he indicated that the street still existed, that unfortunately the house had been bombed in the war and that it had been replaced by an office block; nonetheless, he encouraged me to visit the town of my grandparents.

Now, if this street and number still existed, why were they refusing to supply us with the documentation we requested? I realized we had to proceed carefully and play the bureaucracy at its own game. I asked Angela to find out the names of the firms working in the building. No L'Oréal. We went on with our research. I called the registry once again to ask for a copy of the deeds.

'We only send these documents to the owners or previous owners.'

'But my grandparents owned the property, at least before the war.'

'Their surname?'

'Rosenfelder.'

'No Rosenfelder is mentioned at this address.'

'Go back to the beginning of the century…'

'I've already told you that I went back to the eighteenth century, and particularly from the beginning of this century to the 1940s.'

'But my mother…'

'She made this story up or perhaps they were just tenants. You know, lots of people went slightly mad after what they lived through in the war.'

'Thanks anyway…'

A few days before Christmas 1999, I got another call from my interlocutor at the Prime Minister's Office. He explained how he was going to be the spokesman for a committee that was being set up, that he was a judge and was responsible for my case and that, even though the committee hadn't yet received its rubric, we could fix a meeting early in 2000. I was then rehearsing *Don Giovanni* at the Opéra, and my hours weren't exactly the same as the bureaucracy's.

'I can see you, even if it's late.'

In the event we met one evening after a late rehearsal. I gave him the various bits of information I had managed to extract from my mother by dint of patience and tender care. Of course, she hadn't told me the whole story. I still had work to do because she was resistant. But I couldn't put any more pressure on her; I already felt I was torturing her simply by evoking that period of her life.

I thus learned that after fleeing Karlsruhe in 1938, my grandparents had taken up residence in the eighth *arrondissement*, 6 rue des Saussaies, on the third floor. A large apartment filled with furniture they'd brought with them from Germany. Paintings by the great masters hung on some of the walls. They rented, since Jews didn't have the right to own property by then. My mother had also revealed that my grandfather was an important lawyer. He played the piano and violin brilliantly and had even initially contemplated a career as a conductor, but the wounds he received in the First World War had prevented him from following that route.

I showed the photo of the house to the report-writer.

'Have you written to Karlsruhe to get confirmation that your family lived there?'

'Yes, I even made it plain that the French government was requesting this information. I hope to get a reply soon; I only just sent my letter.'

Several months passed by, I wrote repeatedly, all my letters remained unanswered. I couldn't understand this fresh silence at all. But the ballgame had changed. I had more sway now that I could insist the French government was behind me. I finally picked up my phone to speak directly to the mayor who 'naturally' was unable to take the call. It was his secretary who endured my anger: 'All I want is evidence that my family lived at a specific address in Karlsruhe. I've been requesting a copy of the deeds for years, and now the French government is requesting a copy. I've sent several letters over recent months, and you haven't even deigned to reply. I will take legal action, if needs be!'

'We certainly received your letters. I don't understand what has happened. Here's Mrs V.'

Mrs V. was very embarrassed. Yes, there'd been a mistake: in what way could she be of help? Then she repeated how, in order to get the documentation on the house, one had to contact the land registry.

I felt the Kafkaesque nightmare was resurging: the land registry had been refusing us any documentation at all for years by employing ever more fantastic excuses. I told Mrs V. of the steps I'd taken over the years, that I was desperate and couldn't think what to do next. I told her of the French government's request. I argued that, even if my family had rented this house, they could still send me something that proved they had lived there, anything, an invoice, any scrap of paper... And on that note, I left her my details.

A few hours later, I received a fax that was very difficult to read. I took a magnifying glass and saw the name 'Rosenfelder'. The document, dated 1938, was a Nazi request for a building permission[1] relating to Wendstrasse 19 – the address my mother always mentioned – and carried this information: '*previous owners Isaak and Sophie Rosenfelder née Schnurmann*'. I would later learn that Isaak and Sophie were my great-grandparents, father and mother respectively of Fritz Rosenfelder, my maternal grandfather.

I immediately called Angela: 'I'll send you the fax. Tell me what you can

---

1 The permission was to build a parking lot in the place where the house stood. The document was incomplete and too illegible to see who had made the request. I found that out later, through some cross-referencing.

decipher. I'd like to know if you read there what I read.'

The telephone soon rang: 'How did you get your hands on this?'

I told her quickly, burning to know what she thought.

'Well, yes, it's proof this house belongs to you. It's incredible how they've lied to you for so many years! How could they?'

I called back the land registry, feeling full of energy, and asked the perennial questions of my interlocutor, who was really rude: 'I told you your mother is out of her mind!'

'I'll send you a fax right away.'

I sent him the document and kept my temper.

'You've received it? Perfect. Please send the extracts from the land registry mentioning my family's ownership. You have my address.'

And I hung up.

I received a copy of the extracts a few days later in the post. An apologetic note accompanied the unsigned letter using 'the holidays' as an excuse for the tardiness of the reply.

I quickly read the contents of the extracts. What my eyes could see – even if after several readings I still didn't understand the whole document – was edifying: the name Rosenfelder stood out very clearly[2]. I did not understand why it had been so difficult to get hold of this document. I was soon to find out.

2   See Appendix 1.

4

My Mother

Edith Rosenfelder Waitzfelder is the only daughter of Kaethe and Fritz Rosenfelder. They lived in Karlsruhe, in a magnificent 2,000-square-metre property, Wendstrasse 19. Fritz came from a wealthy family: his mother, Sophie Schnurmann, was the daughter of an industrialist who had prospered in the manufacture and marketing of paper and textiles. Sophie's sister, Cornelia, managed several of the family enterprises. As Cornelia never married, Sophie's children inherited the family patrimony. Max, the eldest, died in the First World War. Karl and Fritz were left. Karl, who was a playwright, left no children. Fritz had one daughter: Edith, my mother, born in July 1928, in the house at Wendstrasse 19.

The position of Jews in Germany started to deteriorate between 1932 and 1934; by the end of 1936, Fritz decided to take his family to Paris in order to escape the Nazi persecutions. Germany was going through a bad period and Paris would provide shelter while they waited for happier times. He knew the city because he had studied there, as well as in London and Geneva. He spoke French and worked as lawyer for the French consulate in Karlsruhe. He went to Paris alone to look for accommodation with the idea of bringing his family over when he had found something. While waiting, he stayed at a hotel, and the family was only reunited in France in September 1938 when it moved to the rue des Saussaies.

But by 1939 Fritz was already being interned in different French prison camps. These included Tence in Haute-Loire, Gurs in the Pyrenees and Les Milles near Marseille. Edith, my mother, Kaethe, my grandmother, and Emma, Kaethe's mother, stayed on at the rue des Saussaies. Edith went to school and played on the Champ-de-Mars.

Fritz had managed to get visas so they could emigrate to the United States, but Emma, who didn't understand what was happening and couldn't imagine the extent of the threat hanging over the family, refused to set off for a country which, according to her, 'had no culture'.

When, in 1941, the situation became untenable in Paris, Kaethe decided to flee with her daughter and mother to an unoccupied area in Allauch, a small village close to Marseille. That was where my mother continued her education. At the very same time Fritz was released from the camp at Les Milles.

In 1942, after a roundup, he was interned again in the camp at Les Milles but this time was on the list of those to be deported to Auschwitz. He managed to escape, but while he was on the run in August 1942, it was his wife Kaethe's turn to be rounded up and sent to Auschwitz where she was gassed to death, then burned in a crematory oven. Miraculously my mother had gone to the beach that day with her teacher and owed her salvation to an intervention by Rosette, a young village girl who arrived before the gendarmes and saved her from being rounded up.

When he learned his wife had been captured and could never return, Fritz worked quickly to recover his daughter, and they reached Switzerland after a perilous crossing of Lake Geneva. There they were first kept in prison before being sent to a refugee camp.

But Fritz was already quite ill; his many long stays in internment camps – cold, locked up and starved of food – had taken their toll of his health. He died on December 31, 1945 in a Geneva hospital.

A large number of the family, cousins, uncles and aunts, who had also sought refuge in France and were then interned, had similarly died of cold or dysentery in the camp at Gurs.

My mother, aged seventeen, found herself alone at the end of the war. She stayed in a refugee camp in Montreux and was fed by a Jewish institution until a responsible relative was found to look after her, as she was still a minor. By the end of 1946, Ernest, an uncle who had emigrated to Sao Paolo, had agreed to take her in. So Edith left for Brazil, not knowing anything about this country's language or culture.

Three months after her twenty-third birthday, she married my father, who lived in Rio de Janeiro. They had two offspring, my brother and I; after our father's death, we have been the ones who see to her needs, for she lives in particularly precarious circumstances.

My mother was prey to great changes of mood. She had moments of pure joy: she told us stories like nobody else, made puppets for us or got out her paint box to sketch our portraits. Then suddenly, quite unexpectedly, she would have periods of melancholy and great sadness that turned her into a quite different woman. She would cry for no reason, and my brother and I took great care not to upset her. We would never talk about such moments at school: children don't like to be different from other children.

Moreover for years I wouldn't let myself cry. I have reneged on that pledge frequently since I started on this process of property reclamation!

The story my mother most liked to tell was the one called 'The Princess and the Pea'. It was her favourite story. My friends often described my mother as a princess. She always kept a noble mien, despite the premature wrinkles. Her face is so lined that when she starts to laugh, one wonders if in fact she isn't really going to cry. L'Oréal beauty creams, very good products all else notwithstanding, have been unable to spare her face the signs of her suffering. On the contrary...

I remember a strange incident – my father told me about it – that happened when they were on their honeymoon in Argentina. My father was a very good dancer and often took my mother out dancing. That evening they had gone to a small village. I don't know what the place can have been like, I don't think there can have been any discotheques at the time, but she suddenly stopped dancing, picked her things up and said she couldn't stay there any longer. She thought she'd spotted Mengele[3] in the

---

3   Dr Josef Mengele, the Nazi doctor in Auschwitz, carried out horrific medical experiments on those held there. He was nicknamed 'the Angel of Death'. He fled to Argentina and it is believed he died in Brazil in 1979.

crowd, and that had reminded her of her mother's death. My father tried to reassure her by saying that Mengele had died with Hitler.

'Don't keep on,' she replied. 'People say he's dead, but I know it's him.'

My father died in 1979 and would never know that, in the 1980s, historians testified to this Nazi criminal's presence in Argentina at that time. There is a strong possibility that he was the man my mother saw.

My mother only returned to Europe twice after leaving Switzerland in 1946. Once with my father, and a second time to visit me. She has nevertheless not forgotten her German roots; whenever friends went to Germany and asked her what she wanted, she used to reply: 'Take a photo of my house, Wendstrasse 19, for me.' One day she was at last sent a present of a very beautiful photo annotated by friends: that's when she discovered L'Oréal had established its German head office there.

My mother really adored France. She had taught French language and literature at the Alliance Française in Rio. When we were small, although we didn't speak a word of French, we would sing nursery rhymes like 'Frère Jacques', 'Alouette, gentille alouette' and many others. We even knew 'La Marseillaise' by heart. My mother listened to Piaf, Montand, Aznavour, Trénet and Barbara. She would talk to us about the *maquis* and the French Resistance fighters who had obtained fake passports for her and her father; they were her heroes.

If they were certainly that, there were many others who borrowed this glorious name at the end of the war: the famous 'last-minute resisters'.

When L'Oréal established itself in Karlsruhe, its reputation was still unblemished. On the contrary, as its arrival in the region coincided with the Allies, the liberators of Europe and conquerors of Nazism, the company enjoyed a more than positive image. L'Oréal belonged to that band of heroes who were about to rebuild the country. One of the Allies's tasks was to ensure that property stolen from the Jews was returned. I was soon to be disenchanted on that front.

5

A Bad-Smelling Perfume

Angela needed the help of another translator and a good four months to complete a first translation of the deeds. As she proceeded with her task, she was shocked by what she uncovered. If some passages still remained opaque, one thing was certain: the house had definitely belonged to the Rosenfelders until 1938, the date when it was 'sold'. The text concerning the 'sale' is not very clear. At the end of the war, the American military government placed an embargo on it – as with all Jewish property purloined by the Nazis – and it was subject to a restitution order. The deeds then signal a new sale to the company, Haarfarben und Parfümerien GmbH.

When I read this name, my mother's phrase immediately echoed in my head: even if L'Oréal wasn't mentioned, it was obviously something related to hair-care products. Perhaps my mother was right. She reacted vociferously when she caught sight of the document: 'You see, I'm not mad! I've been saying that house is mine for sixty years.'

If only for that, the fact that I had recovered this document was a source of satisfaction.

I typed Haarfarben und Parfümerien GmbH into my computer and was able to track the company down very quickly. A few clicks on the Internet were enough to make the link with L'Oréal. I sent my thanks and some sweets to Karlsruhe, in order to thank Mrs V. She called a few days afterwards to thank me, to say that it wasn't necessary, that she was sorry…

'Sorry for what? You did the most one could do for anyone! My mother has been waiting for this document for sixty years. Tell me, Mrs V., how is it possible we've been lied to for so many years when people quite clearly knew this house was ours?'

Mme V. started to whisper: 'You know that before the war things here were done rather.... Equally, after the war, they were done rather deviously[4]. L'Oréal is very important here. I'm sorry. I must hang up. Thank you.'

'I am the one who should be thanking you.'

I felt this story was too much for me. I didn't know what to think or do. Besides, I had operas to study. I hadn't the time to keep everything on the boil.

A few months after the call from the Prime Minister's Office, I went to the CDJC[5] to search for documents related to my grandparents' deportation. En route, I remembered an incident that had occurred six years earlier. I had called the Sons and Daughters of Jewish French Deportees to get any possible information. All I knew then was their name and final destination, Auschwitz. My mother had never said anything to me, so everything else was a great blur for me.

'What was your grandparents' name?'

'Kaethe Rosenfelder, née Hirsch, and Fritz Rosenfelder.'

'Kaethe, train number 29, destination Auschwitz, died in a gas chamber.'

These words cut through my body like a sharp knife, and I hung up at once, distraught. I'd made that call to Serge Klarsfeld's association years ago and now felt strong enough to search out the documents and face their content.

The CDJC employees could only give me the deportation book for my grandmother, Kaethe. They had nothing on her husband, Fritz. They gave me addresses where I could continue my research.

I read and read when I got home. On the first page, the acronyms RF (République française) and SS are printed side by side. The book is

---

4 Mrs V. used the German word '*krumm*'.
5 Centre de documentation juive contemporaine – the Centre for Contemporary Jewish Documentation.

written half in French, half in German. Even though you know what's coming, its content is horrific. It speaks of people as if they were ordinary freight divided up in sections, by age, sex and exit camps. The cargo left on time, so many died on the journey, so many reached their destination, so many passed through the gas chambers. Orders were carried out to the letter, all women died. Only a few men (a number is mentioned) escape immediate death; they will be allocated to forced-labour gangs.

Then come the signatures. It is SS *Sturmbannführer* Hagen who carried out the orders, executing decisions taken at a round table by Eichmann and Laval.

I knew who Eichmann was[6]. When his death was announced my father had declared that it was a day to remember before explaining who this character was. At the time, I didn't try to find out anything else. I went to see one of my neighbours.

'Have you heard of this man Laval?'

She looked at me in astonishment as if I'd asked something quite foolish. Then she remembered I hadn't been brought up in France.

'He was the prime minister in the Vichy government. Why?'

'Because he and Eichmann signed the deportation order for my grandmother. It's strange. I thought only Germans were responsible for the deportation of Jews and that the French government only followed orders. However, it is quite clear they took the decision jointly.'

'Where did your grandparents live?'

'In Paris, 6 rue des Saussaies.'

She sat down when she heard those words.

'What's the matter?'

'The headquarters of the Gestapo was on the rue des Saussaies.'

Then a childhood memory suddenly flashed back: 'Hide, the Gestapo's opposite, hide.' Another sentence I'd heard from my mother's lips. Some things were beginning to make sense.

---

6 Adolf Eichmann (1906–1962), German civil servant, member of the SS, directed the Jewish office at the German High Command. He was in charge of the extermination of all Jews in Europe (the 'Final Solution'). In 1945 he sought refuge in Argentina, but was tracked down by the Israeli police in 1960. He was hanged after a long trial in Jerusalem.

A few days later, I was buying a newspaper when my eyes were drawn to the cover of *L'Express* featuring Liliane Bettencourt, the L'Oréal heiress. The article rather sang her praises. Reference was certainly made to a few shadowy areas darkening the family past, but the point wasn't laboured. I couldn't stop myself from thinking she couldn't be the great lady they described, that her family had taken our house, that we had deliberately – and for many years – been refused access to the deeds mentioning our title deed and that after all that our property had never been returned to us. I'll write to *L'Express*, I told myself, and reveal some other sides to the lady in question. How naive I was!

I called my uncle to tell him what I was planning. He advised me against writing such a letter: I would be challenging powerful people and exposing myself to eventual retaliation. Besides, I didn't know the exact nature of their relationship with the magazine. According to him, even if I were in the right, it would be better to get a lawyer to write the letter. Easy enough to say when you don't mix in this world, when you don't always have the means and you have no time!

Several people commented on the article and asked me questions. I replied timidly that I'd thought of writing to *L'Express*, that I'd been advised to see a lawyer and had finally dropped the whole business.

In fact, I didn't really know which way to turn because some of my friends insisted it was important to do something.

Two months later, I telephoned *Maître* Charles Korman.

6

The Price of a Great Fortune

Born in 1922, Liliane Bettencourt is the daughter and sole heiress of Eugène Schueller, the founder of L'Oréal[7]. She married André Bettencourt in June 1950. The latter met Eugène Schueller at the end of the 1930s. André pursued a political career after the war. Well to the right, he was nonetheless a close, loyal friend of François Mitterand; the two men had met each other and got on well since their youth.

Liliane Bettencourt, with a fortune worth € 14.9 billion[8], is the richest woman in France and occupies thirteenth position in the world ranking of millionaires. According to the Fininfo company, her estimated fortune, including her holdings of stocks and shares, was in the region of $18.4 billion.

And the Bettencourts grow a further € 590,000 richer by the hour, even when they are asleep[9]:

Mme Liliane Bettencourt lives in a large house in Neuilly-sur-Seine, with an array of servants [...] But there is no doubt that the most beautiful of her properties is in Arcouest, in Brittany [...] With its swimming pool full of warm sea water and exquisite view

---

7   Most of the information in this chapter comes from the following books: Emmanuel Faux, Thomas Legrand, Gilles Perez, *La main droite de Dieu: enquête sur François Mitterand et l'extrême droite*, Paris, Le Seuil, 1994, pp. 150-153; and Michel Bar-Zohar, *Une histoire sans fard: L'Oréal des années sombres au boycott arabe*, translated by Serge Moran, Paris, Fayard, 1997, pp. 50-54.

8   *Le Monde*, February 2002.

9   Bruno Abescat, *La Saga des Bettencourt: L'Oréal, une fortune française*, Paris, Plon, 2002, pp. 28, 29.

of the island of Bréhat – that changes at every moment of the day as the tides cover and uncover the rocks – magnificently equipped and sheltered by a clump of eucalyptus trees, the villa enjoys more than a touch of paradise[10].

The Bettencourts mingle with Parisian high society (or perhaps it would be more accurate to say that Parisian high society mingles with the Bettencourts). They enjoy privileged relationships in the political world, on the right and left, starting with successive presidents of the Republic and their wives. Members of the government, of legislative assemblies, the Constitutional Council and the Central Bank pay them court. Beyond political and financial spheres, they have created links in the worlds of media, culture and science; the Bettencourts have established a foundation[11] that sponsors different projects arising from within these same domains. In other words, you can find the Bettencourt touch wherever you probe the decision-making areas in French society.

Eugène Schueller, a chemist, founded L'Oréal in 1907 under the name of the French Company for Harmless Hair Dyes (Société française de teintures innoffensives pour cheveux). The firm quickly prospered, and Schueller found he had a substantial fortune on his hands.

In 1935 he viewed with distaste the probable rise to power of the Popular Front and joined the most extreme nationalist grouping, which loudly proclaimed that it preferred Hitler to the Popular Front. Schueller didn't hesitate to put his wallet where his mouth was and supplied generous support. Thus, from the very start, the CSAR (Secret Committee for Revolutionary Action) sought his help, and it was then that he met its

---

10 Ibid., p. 27.

11 Apart from the founders, Mr and Mrs Bettencourt, their daughter Françoise and son-in-law Jean-Pierre Meyers, the members of the board of this foundation include three well qualified people, ex-directors of L'Oréal – François Dalle, Pascal Castres Saint-Martin and Guy Landon – two representatives belonging to leading state bodies – Michel Albert, inspector of finances and member of the National Institute of France, and Jean-Luc Silicani, state counsellor – and finally three upstanding members – Jean-Pierre Duport, Prefect for the Île-de-France, Prefect of Paris, Professor of Medicine Alain Pompidou and businessman Marc Ladreit de Lacharrière, also a former collaborator with L'Oréal and now occupying the position of treasurer.

founder, Eugène Deloncle. The group, which met several times at L'Oréal headquarters, 14 rue Royale in Paris, soon became very famous under the name of La Cagoule – 'The Hood'. Schueller was not happy merely investing large sums of money in this clandestine organization that championed violent action: he was one of its most outlandish ideologues.

There was another key man in La Cagoule: Jacques Corrèze, Deloncle's assistant. His codename was *la Bûche* –'The Log'. He was involved in most of the bloody actions or murders committed by La Cagoule before the war. In fact, no sooner was it created than the organization embarked on a series of political murders. A villa in Rueil harboured a strong-room and torture chamber. Poison was stolen from research institutes in order to suppress traitors to the cause. Four aeroplanes on their way to Spain exploded in flight. In Paris, two bombs destroyed the buildings of the General Confederation of French Industry and the Inter-professional Employers Union, in an attempt to lay blame for the attacks on the Communists.

Moreover, to support the *coup d'état* it was preparing against the Republic, the organization assembled an impressive stockpile of arms. Thousands of hand grenades, hundreds of rifles and machine guns and munitions were seized in their Paris warehouse.

In 1937 the organization walked straight into a trap set by the police, who spread the rumour that the Communists were preparing an insurrection in Paris. The 'red' threat mobilized almost all the members of La Cagoule, and the police, under the orders of Marx Dormoy, Minister of the Interior, arrested fifty-seven of them. Schueller escaped, but Deloncle wasn't so lucky. But he wouldn't stay long behind bars: the war and the Occupation soon put an end to judicial investigations.

The defeat in 1940 and advent of the Pétain government were a godsend for La Cagoule; it could finally become enmeshed in the structures of power. Thus, in Vichy, from among the leading members of La Cagoule, François Méténier was put in charge of the armed groups protecting the head of the National Revolution; Gabriel Jeantet was Marshal Pétain's right-hand man; and Colonel Goussard his loyal follower. He would in the end join the Resistance.

In Paris, Deloncle openly collaborated with the Gestapo and the SS via a legal avatar of La Cagoule, the Movement for Social Revolution (Mouvement social révolutionnaire, or MSR) founded with Schueller in September 1940. The names of the two men appeared side by side on posters, tracts and invitations. The first manifesto of the movement – entitled 'Revolution! MSR. Resurrection!' – included the signatures of, among others, Deloncle, Schueller and Corrèze. The latter was a member of its political bureau as was that veteran *cagoulard*, Jean Filliol. The MSR officially published its chain of command. Schueller was part of the executive committee as chair of all the technical committees. The secretariat for these committees was established at L'Oréal headquarters, 14 rue Royale[12].

The MSR was an umbrella for two organizations that trumpeted anti-Semitic battle cries: the Anti-Jewish Movement and the French Community, to which Corrèze belonged. This gentleman requested and engineered the setting up of a General Commissariat for Jewish Questions (Commissariat général aux questions juives, or CGJQ) that then became the Institute for the Study of Jewish Questions (l'Institut d'étude des questions juives, or IEQJ) directed by a man by the name of Sézille. On April 5 1941, Sézille wrote to Deloncle: 'The MSR must and will be the executive arm and the French Community, through its sphere of study and documentation, will provide the means.' And, when the IEQJ created its anti-Jewish brigades in July 1941, the MSR was responsible for remunerating the district leaders[13].

But the time had come for the MSR to expand its base and enhance its status from a group to that of a party. Under the approving gaze of the German Embassy, it published a violently anti-Semitic, anti-democratic and racist platform before merging with another pro-Nazi organization led by Marcel Déat in order to set up the National Popular Assembly (Rassemblement national populaire, or RNP) the Parisian secretary of which was none other than Corrèze.

---

12 See Appendices 17 and 18.
13 Anti-Jewish services were concentrated at 11 rue des Saussaies.

The RNP programme was as follows: 'Our goal is to pursue, in a planned, methodical way, the exclusion of the Jews and to defend the interests of the French damaged by the Jews.' In the course of the first RNP Congress in June 1941, one speaker after another took to the podium to encourage the French to 'cleanse the country of Jews and its latest bastard offspring, Gaullism'. Schueller, head of the RNP technical committees, described the three axes of the economic revolution to be carried through: wages, management and capital. For the revolution to succeed he harangued his audience, 'we must quickly execute fifty or a hundred important people'.

Intoxication with power didn't mean La Cagoule forgot its former enemies: in July 1941, the former Minister of the Interior, Marx Dormoy, paid with his life for having defused the plot they were hatching before the war. A bomb was placed under his pillow. When La Cagoule went on trial, the official report of which I managed to track down, a witness declared that Deloncle and the leadership of La Cagoule ordered this attack.

Marx Dormoy was not the only man to suffer the murderous vengeance of La Cagoule. As if the blood already spilt wasn't enough to appease it, Deloncle – who still needed so sorely to prove to the Occupier that he was a genuine collaborator – had seven synagogues blown up on the night of 2 October.

In the aftermath of the war, L'Oréal was there to allow former collaborators and a number of *cagoulards* to discreetly restore their virginity. Thus, Jacques Corrèze (*cagoulard* number 552) secretary general of the MSR and involved in the LVF[14] resurfaced in the Spanish branch of L'Oréal, then became President of Cosmair, the branch of L'Oréal in the United States. Jean Filliol (*cagoulard* number 43), the main thug in La Cagoule, was taken on under the pseudonym of André Lamy. Gabriel Jeantet (*cagoulard* number 467) and Jean Leguay were also recruited. For the record, the latter – Bousquet's assistant at the General Secretariat for the Police in the Occupation and representative for the Secretariat in the

---

14 Légion des volontaires français – the Legion of French Volunteers.

Northern region – is considered to be one of those with most responsibility for the Vél d'Hiv[15] roundup.

At the time of the Liberation, Schueller employed François Mitterand, making him Executive Director of Editions du Rond-Point (a L'Oréal financed activity). He encouraged him to get involved in politics, and it was L'Oréal that financed his first campaign. Very soon after he was elected a deputy in November 1946, Schueller's young protégé received his first ministerial portfolio[16].

---

15 On 16 and 17 July 1942 more than 8,000 Jews including 4,000 children were gathered in the Vélodrome d'Hiver in Paris in atrocious conditions. Organized by the French police, this roundup was one of the most important acts of anti-Semitic persecution committed by the French authorities.

16 E. Faux, T. Legrand, G. Perez, *La Main droite de Dieu: enquête sur François Mitterand et l'extrême droite*, pp. 150–153.

7

Rheingold

Maître Korman gave me an appointment on 21 December 2000. In January I was leaving, first for a few days in Budapest then to Toulouse as assistant producer for *Das Rheingold*, the first volet of Wagner's trilogy. Subsequently, after two days in Paris, I would be off again, this time to Bilbao for Donizetti's *Lucia di Lammermoor*. It was the only possible date before March.

I started to tell him my story. I had brought the article from *L'Express* and told him of my intention to write to the magazine. I think he wasn't too sure whether to believe me or not, but my tale interested him, particularly the way I told it. By then I'd managed to collect the Nazi building permission from 1938, the extract from the Karlsruhe land registry (*Grundbuch*), my grandmother's deportation book, my own birth certificate, where it noted that Kaethe and Fritz Rosenfelder are my maternal grandparents, that of my mother who was born in Karlsruhe, my grandparents' marriage certificate and documents showing, first, that my grandfather was imprisoned in several camps and was on the deportation list from the camp in Les Milles, and second, that the Rosenfelder family had lived at 6 rue des Saussaies, in Paris. Finally, I showed him the fruits of my research on the Internet and the links I'd found between Haarfarben und Parfümerien and L'Oréal.

But all that wasn't enough for my interlocutor; he wanted still more. I couldn't hide a degree of irritation.

'I have only come to see you in order to write a letter. Please tell me if that will be at all possible. Yes or no?'

'More documentation is needed. And we can do much better than just write a letter.'

I have always mistrusted lawyers and immediately felt defensive.

'Do you want to get your house back? Yes or no?'

His suggestion was tempting, but I found it difficult to believe. He then proposed that I continue my research and find out more about the links between Haarfarben und Parfümerien and L'Oréal. How would I find such information? I didn't know where to start. I left him saying that I would think about it.

Despite all the difficulties, the conversation had rekindled my spirits. I called Angela to ask her to carry out more research. There were perhaps other facts to dig out of a library or some other institution. She was spurred on; we were now into our tenth year of investigations.

I was in Budapest when she told me that she had perhaps found something in an archive service. Fearing we would face opposition when we tried to get a copy, we acted as if we were research students. We received a document from 1961, an extract from a company register mentioning L'Oréal, rue Royale, in Paris, and Liliane Bettencourt as shareholders in Haarfarben und Parfümerien (other shareholders were listed with their respective holdings). Address: Wendstrasse 19.

It was more grist to my mill. All the more so because there was also mention of a building of great value and of the bank with which the company was working: the Dresdner Bank.

I called my lawyer to tell him of my discoveries. He then asked me to get an estimate of the building's value. That seemed a daunting undertaking as work was absorbing all my energies: *Das Rheingold* is a demanding opera that requires lots of time and energy. Rehearsals gave way to dress rehearsals, and I would never get back to my hotel bedroom in Toulouse before midnight.

Angela, whom I'd told about my lawyer's new request, called me a few weeks later. She had found a kind of figure that gave more or less the rental price of property by the square metre in Germany and by sector. But there was no such information on sale prices. So we started to research the cost of property in the district that concerned us.

Meanwhile, I had meticulously studied the deeds, noted that there were 700 square metres of land and that the house had three floors as well as a basement (My mother always said the house was 2,000 square metres). Thus, I was able to make my first rough estimates, but the price I came up with was so startling that I had to do the calculations several times over to make sure I'd not made a mistake. I like to think I'm pretty good at maths, but suddenly I doubted myself. I called a neighbour in Paris, who is an accountant; my figures were correct. I passed these figures on to *Maître* Korman. We set up a meeting for the end of February, on my return.

I had also re-established contact with Mrs V. at the Karlsruhe town hall. I wanted to know if L'Oréal still owned the building and, if not, who did. This time it was several weeks before I received a reply: the person who worked at the land registry had left but had been replaced. According to her, L'Oréal no longer owned the building, although she wasn't at all certain. She was far from convinced.

'L'Oréal is still very powerful here,' she told me.

I stopped contacting her to avoid creating any more difficulties for her and finally decided to call the new person administrating the registry. It was a blessing. *A priori*, I had no idea with whom I would be dealing, I was walking on eggshells.

'I'm not the substitute, but the person now in charge of the service. How can I help you?'

Mr Müller's tone voice was quite different to his predecessor's; one sensed his courage and frankness.

'No, Madame, L'Oréal no longer owns the building. You know, it is a very large building.'

'Who does own it now?'

'The State and the Land of Bade-Würtemberg.'

'Can you send me a copy of the bill of sale?'

'No problem at all.'

On my return to Paris, I found the document in my post box. L'Oréal had sold the building in 1991 for DM5.3 million, then rented part to the new owner for the two months following the sale. What a godsend! I didn't even need to ask for expert advice: all the figures were there for the sale and the rental. Besides, a basement was mentioned and, when a building is 580 square metres at ground level, one imagines the basement is not a negligible space. I know how valuable it is to have such an extension in a coveted neighbourhood.

When I met up with my lawyer armed with these documents, I felt he took me a little more seriously. But, although he appreciated the fruits of my research, he still wasn't satisfied. I learned, after three months of interacting with him, that he rarely pays compliments in a meeting and that *Maître* Korman prefers to point his finger at the tasks still to be completed: a tactic designed to drive me mad. I advanced several hypotheses.

'That is possible, but I want proof.'

'But how will I find them? Do you realize what you are asking me to do?'

'You will find them.'

And that's all there is to it!

8

Os Gringos

My parents were gringos in the eyes of Brazilians. My mother will always retain this slightly pejorative nickname Brazilians give to foreigners: she speaks Portuguese with a French accent.

I'm not at all a *gringa*: I was born in Brazil. Nonetheless, from my early childhood, I've always felt a bit foreign. Even with the ease of communication that comes with the ability to speak several languages, this feeling continues to haunt me wherever I go.

I learned to recite the alphabet by heart in my English school. Then I went to a Brazilian school and, when I had to recite it, I'd first think it through in English before my small child's head translated it into Portuguese at top speed. I worked that way for years, 'through translation' – and not only in order to recite the alphabet; I had to adapt my behaviour continuously in order to be in step with the new realities I confronted.

Children, it's well known, want above everything to be like everybody else. At a very early age we already spoke three languages, and our mother wasn't at all like the mothers of our playmates. The difference could also be felt within the Jewish community. Several friends of my mother had also lost their nearest of kin in the camps or had been robbed. But they had all received compensation for the Shoah. Even if money were no replacement for what had disappeared, it at least had this merit: their suffering had been officially recognized. Justice had been done, and each in his or her own way had been able to turn the page.

It was quite another story with my mother. We didn't know whether her grief made her transgress the frontiers of truth. If what she affirmed was true, then why couldn't she produce documentation like other people? Why hadn't she received compensation? In the face of the doubts hovering over her, she learned not to go out on a limb, to keep quiet and pretend to be the same as everybody else. And we, her children, followed her example and in turn erected our own façades. Thus, because I felt different from my companions, I had no choice but to 'translate' in order to be understood by them.

I remember that at home our passports, together with a small suitcase, were always at the ready, to cope with any eventuality. That was how it had to be, my parents needed that to feel calm. Also the house was a real grocery store, and as soon as our reserves began to run out, my mother would rush to the shops. My brother was amused by her behaviour and couldn't stop himself from remarking ironically that we had enough to feed the whole of Napoleon's army.

My mother wasn't the only one to act in this way: all her friends who had experienced the war did the same. Cupboards and refrigerators were always full to bursting. And, as if this weren't enough, my mother would bake two or three cakes a day. But I remember the delights of her cooking as well as her compulsive behaviour. She was a real *cordon bleu*, and tasty teas always followed the French lessons she taught groups of pupils at home; her chocolate mousse and other dishes were appreciated by one and all.

Jews who didn't lose any member of their family in the Shoah don't have the slightest idea about the universe inhabited by those who weren't so fortunate. Death, for anyone who has never lost a loved one, is an abstract idea. No words can make anyone understand. The same goes for the emptiness and pain that accompany us. What a strange feeling it is to sense at your side a poignant presence singling you out from other people. It is something you'd like to throw off but will never be able to, and you wonder in the end whether one day it will in fact stop.

While I have been reconstructing my family's history, this presence has moreover allowed me to understand, not intellectually but almost physically, the causes of wars, at the risk of seeming ingenuous yet again.

The reasons invoked are never those really motivating war-makers. Similarly, the 'saviours' use the pretext of coming to help those attacked when in fact they are only thinking about their own interests: in the first place money, but also fame, indirect advantage and the sharing out of power. Of course, amid the naked predators, there are fortunately people whose only wish is to serve the common interest, but their number remains decidedly small.

We celebrated Sabbath on Friday evening. My parents weren't particularly religious but, good Brazilians that we were, we liked to have a party, whether it was Jewish or not. Thus, we would pray the prayer of bread, wine and lights around the table laid with a white tablecloth where the dishes prepared by my mother had pride of place. We never answered the telephone during the meal and if one of us was meeting a friend that evening, that friend was invited to dine. We celebrated Hanukkah as it should be celebrated. The celebrations of Rosh Hashana, Yom Kippur and Passover were livelier: more than twenty guests would sit around the table when these festivities were held at our house.

Christian celebrations like Christmas, Twelfth Night or Easter gave us an opportunity to visit our friends, who were generally Catholic and came to our house for Sabbath and our special days.

My mother adored having people around her. It was her way of redressing the emptiness created by a total absence of family on her side. My father believed in God, my mother didn't. She said that if God existed, He wouldn't allow certain things to happen.

My brother and I adored one celebration more than any other: it was the Succot or Feast of the Tabernacles, because all the children living in the street were invited into our own home. On this occasion, my father would build a large hut with fruit and vegetables. We had the right to eat from it (you only had to stretch out a hand to serve yourself) and sleep there.

So our parents passed on to us certain traditions before giving us the freedom later to continue with them or not. Today I only join in these celebrations when I return to Brazil where my mother still keeps on with them. Nevertheless, in France I do go to the synagogue to say Kaddish during Yom Kippur, in memory of my father who asked me to do so from his deathbed. Each year, I make use of this moment to step outside my hectic life and reflect. I think of my father lovingly but sometimes also sadly. I ponder certain aspects of my existence, and I still experience the same pleasure hearing the sound of the shofar in the Parisian synagogue I go to. I remember how there was a resounding organ and choir in Rio. The music alone was enough to make us want to go to the synagogue: it was beautiful and moreover was played by excellent musicians.

One year, at the time of the Yom Kippur festivities, they began to read out loudly the names of all the members of the congregation who had died in the extermination camps. Each name echoed like a hammer blow in my ears. I felt I was suffocating and couldn't continue listening. I left the synagogue.

From time to time we would go to the countryside, to Itaipava, and stay in a house we rented with other families. The countryside, in Brazil, is the forest. A huge forest with exuberant vegetation. We liked to be in contact with it and feel the earth under our feet penetrating our bodies, reminding us that life was there. This closeness to the forest was a great source of comfort in periods when my mother was unwell.

Music had its place in the countryside: we performed accordion concerts for ourselves. Forty of us would play on our accordions tunes like 'La Dame aux camélias', while a young girl, dressed all in blue, carried a big basket of equally blue flowers that she threw to the audience. It was very kitsch, but I loved it.

9

Unterdruckverkauf

I am not the kind of person to leave things half-done. If what I've started isn't finished, it's not my style to stop mid-flow. So I read and reread the deeds and found fresh clues each time. But a few passages still eluded me.

The owner of the Internet café where I go to do administrative chores had spoken to me several times about L'Oréal's dark past. My lawyer and I had also discussed this, but without making any headway. I was advised in this respect to make contact with the World Jewish Congress. At the mere mention of the name L'Oréal, their interest was immediately aroused, but the person I had to consult was travelling. While I waited for him to return, I tried my luck with the CDJC. Perhaps I would glean some information there. I would!

'Have you never heard about the L'Oréal affair?'

'Vaguely.'

I began to read the documents they gave me. I was taken aback. The first thing that struck me was the correlation of dates. L'Oréal, through its chief executive François Dalle, was accused of 'racial discrimination' towards Jews, in the wake of a scandal – the Frydman affair[17] – which broke in 1991, the date when the group was selling its property in Karlsruhe. The first revelations in this scandal dated back to 1989: the same year that negotiations had begun for the sale of Wendstrasse 19.

---

17 See Chapter 18.

There is one fact related to this I have yet to mention: the bill of sale Mr Müller sent me in 1991 had come together with appendices containing letters signed by a minister and members of the cabinet giving their consent[18].

I was too shocked to read to the end of the documents I'd been given. I made photocopies and went to Fayard the publishers to buy two copies of book on the affair (one for my lawyer)[19].

Each page rang bells for me. There were so many things in common between what I was reading and my family's history that they couldn't be mere coincidences. I discovered that Eugène Schueller, the founder of L'Oréal, had also been one of the founder members of La Cagoule, that Fascist, anti-Semitic organization from the 1930s which used to meet…on the corner of the rue des Saussaies. In other words, at the very time my grandmother Kaethe, her mother Emma and my mother Edith left their home on the rue des Saussaies to flee to the unoccupied territory in Allauch, near Marseille.

When I reached this point in my research, I realized that it was in 1991 that L'Oréal had sought to rid itself of a property linking it to its notoriously anti-Semitic past.

I finally met up with my adviser at the World Jewish Congress. His family was also originally from Karlsruhe. When he saw the documents I had brought, including the title deeds certifying that my family was the owner of Wendstrasse 19, he assured me that I could try to take L'Oréal to court. My lawyer and I had already discussed this possibility. My first reaction was not to go on a war footing; I much prefer peaceful solutions, and negotiation seemed to me to be much more appropriate. If we were dealing with reasonable people, we might be able to reach an amicable settlement. All the more so given that the anti-Semitic fervour of one generation does not condemn *a priori* the next. Besides, it wasn't my style to condemn anyone without giving them a right of reply, I told myself: 'Let's give them a chance!'

---

18 Note that the State and the Land were presenting themselves as purchasers.
19 Michel Bar-Zohar, *Une histoire sans fard: L'Oréal des années sombres au boycott arabe.*

So we began to prepare a letter to L'Oréal refining the calculations of the amount of total compensation I could claim in my family's name. While so doing, I couldn't help but think of all those years my mother had spent without that money which was hers by right – and which she had sorely lacked.

But let's go back to the documentation – in particular, the title deeds – for we are still only beginning to find things out.

We noticed that Angela had made a mistake in the translation of the title deeds. She had translated 'Madischer Gemeinde' when she should have read 'Badischer Gemeinde'. In her defence, the document is barely legible at this point and I myself had confused the letters M and B[20]. Anyway, it was a reference to the Badischer Gemeinde Versicherung Verband (BGV), an insurance company working for local companies in the Baden region. It was then we realized that this firm had appropriated the house in 1938.

My lawyer asked me to reconstruct the history of this company. How could I? I was on the road again. I found it on the Internet but followed through by phone: I called Mr Müller in Karlsruhe and begged him to inform me as to the existence of a bill of sale from 1938. Yes, it existed, and Mr Müller sent it me.

The seal of the Third Reich[21] figures to the left of the signature on the deed of transfer. And, to my amazement, there is a power of attorney from my grandfather. The power of attorney authorizes one Luise Dürr to carry out all legal or juridical acts on his behalf and gives these acts the same validity as if he had carried them out himself, to dispose of all his property and even to transfer all his rights to a third person. And it all remained valid after his death. Although it doesn't specify for how many generations...[22]

No one in his right mind, even less so a leading lawyer like my grandfather, could have signed such a document except under constraint. Fritz was in Paris when he signed this permission at the German consulate,

20 See Appendix 1.
21 See Appendix 5.
22 See Appendix 4.

while his wife Kaethe, daughter (my mother) and mother-in-law Emma were still in Karlsruhe.

There is a term in German to describe these forced concessions made under the Third Reich: *Unterdruckverkauf* – sale under constraint.

After reading these facts, what else was there to say but that it was quite obvious the story stank to high heaven. I then asked Mr Müller to send me the deed of purchase of Wendstrasse 19 by Haarfarben und Parfümerien (L'Oréal). Reading this deed, dated 1954, brought a fresh surprise: there it stated in black and white that after the war the house was subject to the provisions for the process of restoring Jewish property to their former Jewish owners. But, by the side of this observation, the Nazis who had bestowed the property upon themselves in 1938 stipulate between apostrophes that 'the case has been closed'. Everything is in order. Period.[23]

There is another quite shocking side to this document: L'Oréal gave over the war compensation to the seller, Badischer Gemeinde Versicherung Verband (BGV): in other words, to the Nazis who had appropriated the house in 1938. These indemnities should have come to my mother, the woman who inherited this house. And I just think how over the years my mother has been told when asked why she had no right to war compensation: 'It's been awarded already.' But they forgot to specify to her that it had in fact been awarded to the Nazis who'd taken her house from her in the first place. In the event, L'Oréal purchased the house for DM27,000[24].

We thus sent a letter to L'Oréal on 18 June 2001: the property that had belonged to them had been stolen in the Nazi era and they were still enjoying the fruits of this robbery. Consequently, we were seeking reparations for this injustice, and they were given a month in which to reply. My lawyer and I decided to make it clear we favoured the path of conciliation but that in case of refusal we would appeal to the courts.

We also wrote, of course, to the German BGV insurance company as well as to the Versorgung des Bundes und der Länder, the present owners of Wendstrasse 19.

23 See Appendix 6.
24 Or some € 13,200.

The reply from L'Oréal reached my lawyer on 13 July 2001, five days before the expiry of the deadline. The letter, dated the twelfth, is signed by Lindsay Owen-Jones, chief executive of L'Oréal. The Shoah was an absolute tragedy as far as he was concerned, he wrote, but as a company L'Oréal did not believe it had done any wrong to Mme Edith Rosenfelder and he gave us the names of their lawyers who could provide 'a legally irrefutable analysis of the situation'.

10

Rue des Saussaies

I finally decided to see what my grandparents' apartment might have looked like on the rue des Saussaies. Merely consulting my map of Paris to find the nearest métro station had made me nervous. 'Champs-Élysées-Clemenceau' had been up to then the station where I got out to see art exhibitions at the Grand Palais.

When I came out of the métro, I noted the unusual nature of the residential buildings in the area. I asked the man at the newspaper kiosk for the way, and he directed me towards the Élysée Palace, home to the president of the Republic. Convinced he hadn't understood me, I asked several people the same question and got the same reply. So I walked past the Élysée to the place Beauvau, where the rue des Saussaies starts. 'Place Beauvau' rang a bell. Under the tricolour flag of the French Republic, a group of uniformed men was guarding a building. I asked one of them.

'It's the Ministry of the Interior.'

Of course! What a fool I was.

I crossed the street and couldn't stop shaking when I saw number 6. I went back to the pavement opposite in order to get a better view and saw that the Ministry of the Interior was exactly opposite number 6. The latter is a three-storied building with bedrooms under the eaves. I waited for someone to go in because you needed an entry code, then I went up to the third floor and rang. No response. I went down to the ground floor and explained to the person who had let me in that my grandparents lived there during the war. She said the flat was up for sale, gave me the details of the estate agency and allowed me to visit hers, specifying that the one on the third floor was bigger, some 180 square metres. After leaving the building, I took another look round: the Élysée Palace, then the Ministry of the Interior. In 1944, André Bettencourt worked at the Ministry of the Interior.

Shortly afterwards, I received a very kind letter from the Pyrénées-Atlantiques Regional Authorities. They had discovered a document that related to the interning of my grandfather in the camp in Gurs. It originated from the police in Lyons.

For the first time in my life I had a physical description of my grandfather: one metre eighty-five tall and blue-eyed. And a redhead like me. The document also mentioned the wounds he'd received to his right arm and leg in the First World War. I knew he had had a special violin made so he could play it with the bow in his left hand, and that his favourite pieces were the Bach Partitas for solo violin.

He also loved opera, notably Wagner and, another nod from destiny, I'd been working on a production of Wagner operas ever since that first meeting with my lawyer; and that brought me close to my grandfather again.

What a pity I never knew him. I would love us to have played together. I can imagine we'd have enjoyed some lively, passionate arguments. We wouldn't have always been in agreement as to particular interpretations or conductors, but agreed or not, we'd have compared reactions and sometimes ended up laughing ourselves silly.

Apart from music, my grandfather was fond of painting. Research I have carried out into the paintings he owned prove at least one thing: he found a place for contemporary art on his walls.

As for my grandmother, I'd seen a photo of her in a book that mentions our family in Germany and its deportation. I have the same eyes as her. Her face radiates sweetness and tenderness but also character. She was clearly a beautiful woman. She wasn't yet thirty when this photo was taken. She wasn't yet forty when she died.

When I think of my grandparents, I start imagining what our life might have been like if they were still alive. We might be in the grand rooms in their Karlsruhe villa for, if my grandfather had survived, he wouldn't have let anyone take his house from him. But perhaps we might have been on the rue des Saussaies talking politics or commenting on the actions of the successive occupants of the nearby Élysée Palace or place Beauvau. We would constitute a normal family.

On the other hand, I find it difficult to imagine what my relationship might have been with my grandmother Kaethe. I know nothing about her. My mother never mentioned her. She says she doesn't remember. Did she like music? Did she play an instrument? Did she like dancing? Reading? Was she a good cook? So many unanswered questions. A total void, nothingness. All I have to hang on to is what emanates from that photo where her gaze gives the impression that she enjoyed a rich inner life.

11

Indignation

Lindsay Owen-Jones, the then L'Oréal CEO, speaks of a 'legally irrefutable analysis of the situation' in his letter of 12 July. My lawyer had just read it to me, and he found it hard to restrain my anger:

'*Maître*, the only thing that is irrefutable in this situation is the following, that house belonged to the Rosenfelders and my mother, Fritz Rosenfelder's sole heir, never signed a deed of sale or anything delegating that to anyone else. This letter doesn't stand up, and I'm beginning to think these people are dishonest.'

'Do you know which lawyers they have hired?'

'No, you tell me.'

'*Maîtres* Jean Veil and Michel Zaoui[25]. They are the people I must deal with.'

'I'm sorry, I know the opera world, but not the world of the courts.'

'Jean Veil is Simone Veil's son.'

Of course, I knew who Simone Veil was and was astonished by what I had just heard.

'A Jew defending people who deny Jews their rights in relation to the Nazi theft of their property? I can't believe it! His own mother was a prisoner in a camp! It can't be right whichever way you look at it!'

---

25 See Appendix 9.

'That's not all, Michel Zaoui is a member of the executive committee of the CRIF[26]. He was even one of the lawyers for the civil plaintiffs in the Barbie, Touvier and Papon trials.'

'Is this possible, ethically speaking? I don't know what is worse about what you've just told me. I need time to think.'

I rang the World Jewish Congress. At first, they didn't react. Then, once they'd got over their surprise, they told me that if these lawyers had accepted this job, it was to enable me to negotiate a better deal: that could be the only reason. Everyone else I spoke to gave a similar answer. Despite such reassuring observations, I felt sick and was ready to throw up.

My mother chose that moment to telephone. She sensed I was not well, and finally I told her why. She has seen every shade and hue in life and simply commented: 'Why should you think Jews are different to other people? There are good people, and people who are not so good, among Jews as with everybody else. Do you think there are no Jewish murderers, thieves or traitors? There's a bit of everything. And do you think they were all wonderful in the camps?'

'It's true, there were "traitors" in the camps[27].'

'Yes. And I'm not trying to make excuses for them – there are no excuses – but at the time those traitors were risking their lives. Today, as far as I know, nobody is risking his life. Don't let them beat you down. The directors of L'Oréal have done this on purpose; don't play their game.'

'It makes me sick! What a confusion of roles! Defending the victims in the morning and their likely executioners in the afternoon!'

'After all they've done to stop me from recovering my house, do you think they will let go just like that? You should remember that Nazi philosophy has always been to pit one Jew against another. As far as I'm

---

26 Conseil représentatif des institutions juives de France – the Representative Council of Jewish Institutions in France. I discovered subsequently that he was also president of the legal committee of LICRA (Ligue internationale contre le racisme et l'antisémitisme – the International League against Racism and anti-Semitism).

27 Jews allotted by Nazis to supervise other prisoners in the concentration camps. By agreeing to do this they saved their own lives. They often had the task of putting bodies in the ovens.

concerned, those two are not Jews, at least not in the way I identify and respect those that are mine. They know that the house is ours just as much as we do. I recognize these techniques because I've lived them in my flesh. I'm only sorry you have to relive this. But the fact that L'Oréal has chosen two Jewish lawyers shows they've got a guilty conscience.'

One can defend the fact that Jewish lawyers work for L'Oréal. Life goes on, and if Jews refused to work with all enterprises which had collaborated with the Nazis or which had a dishonourable past, life would get very complicated.

What really shocks me is that these lawyers are defending L'Oréal in a case that specifically has to do with the impact of Nazi policy on Jews. Men like Eugène Schueller who are personally involved in our story have actively implemented this policy on their own behalf. He was hounded because of his past as a collaborator after the war and only escaped being sentenced because of the political connections of his future son-in-law André Bettencourt with François Dalle, a future chief executive of L'Oréal, and François Mitterand, a close friend of these two.

I spent a week recovering morally and physically. Only then could I stand back and understand what my mother had said. It restored my energy to carry on fighting.

We were at the end of July 2001, and my lawyer was leaving for his holidays. As for me, I was still waiting for this famous irrefutable proof in order to decide what step to take next: if they persisted in hiding the truth, we would take them to court.

The month of August turned out to be very fruitful.

The first days were quiet. I stayed in Paris for I had to prepare the restaging of a past production of *Rigoletto* at l'Opéra-Bastille for the early autumn (rehearsals began at the end of August).

In the middle of August, my lawyer called to say he had received a reply from the BGV (the Badischer Gemeinde Versicherung Verband insurance company which had 'bought' the house in 1938). Their letter indicated that the litigious sale of 1938 had been settled in 1951 via a Jewish organization — which no longer exists — that was dedicated to the restitution of stolen Jewish property. So the company was not implicated in the problem we were raising. It enclosed a copy of the so-called agreement with an accompanying letter that mentioned the fact that Karl Rosenfelder (my great-uncle, Fritz's brother) had signed this agreement.

But you can spend a long time looking for my great-uncle's signature on this document: you won't find it[28]. Nor will you find the least mention of the existence of my mother, the direct heir to my grandparents. How could they silence her existence or, worse, give the impression that she was dead, when in fact she had survived the Shoah?

I was indignant but had to be clear in my own mind: I faxed this document to my mother. That put her in a right state. But I persisted, risked being insulted by her and asked whether she'd ever signed a document, by proxy… Brazil is a long way from France, but I felt she was going to come down the line at me her reaction was so violent: how could I doubt her in this way?

'Mum, I don't doubt what you say, but I must confirm what I already know. To have the strength to continue, I must be sure of my ground.'

She blasted down the line: '*That house is mine*, and any document which states the contrary is a lie or the result of subterfuge. How can they pretend to know better than I what I have or haven't done? Isn't what they've already put me through enough? No! *I never signed a thing*, and they should stop their charades. If they think I am senile, they are mistaken. One never forgets things like that.'

I wasn't unhappy to hear her protest vociferously after so many years of resignation.

'I'm sorry, Mum, I didn't want to hurt you.'

'You're not going to get like them, are you?'

'Of course not, I just need to be sure.'

She understood me. It was becoming clearer and clearer there was something devious in this story or '*krumm*' to repeat the word used by Mrs V. at the Karlsruhe town hall. But what? And how was I going to get at it?

28 See Appendix 8.

12

The Little She-Devil

I have always been a bundle of energy. As a child, my father found me so restless that he nicknamed me *Teufelle* or *Diaba*: little she-devil. He would say I was only angelic when asleep. That made me furious, but he never called me by my first name. Later on, the men I've lived with have had to cope with that; on the one hand, they found it stimulating, on the other I made their lives impossible.

But this excess of energy makes me feel that I exist. They say that people who have no history feel they have been deprived of the right to exist. I think it was what happened to my mother; and we, her children, have inherited her state. In order to grow, a family needs its history, as a plant needs its roots.

But L'Oréal deprived us of this vital base. I have experienced each of its negations of the truth as one more refusal of our right to exist. And I'm certain I will never regain that right until justice has given us back our property or the fruits from that property. Before the Nazis even programmed the extermination of the Jews, their policy was to take their rights away from them. If we can't reclaim our rights, it would mean they had won, in spite of history.

The word 'fruits' has a deeper sense for me. I have always wanted to have children. To no avail. Physically, everything is fine; I had every test possible and nothing abnormal was ever found but I was left feeling confused.

People have told me how the feeling of non-existence might have prevented me from having children because to create them, one must exist. I am only now beginning to understand the significance of this theory.

My brother hasn't had children either. My mother did. True, but she had them before she knew she would be denied her past and that her history would be stolen from her; at that time, she was convinced she was going to recover her property after the war like the majority of Jews in her situation.

My mother has never understood why death spared her. I think the fact she survived has weighed her down terribly; she felt guilty. In her moments of anguish, she would repeat the following phrase like a litany: '*Gerichtet nein geretet*' (Judged, not saved). I only discovered much later, thanks to my profession, that this was from the final exchange in the first part of Goethe's *Faust*:

MEPHISTOFELES: She is judged!

VOICE (from on high):   She is saved!

And Marguerite goes to Heaven.

My mother never spoke to me about Kaethe before I started my research into the house in Karlsruhe. So I knew nothing about my grandmother's death. Through studying *Faust*, I understood that if my mother never mentioned her, she nonetheless knew everything there was to know. I would even go so far as to say: it was because she knew everything that she never mentioned her.

I have tried several times to broach issues to do with the war: it is astonishing how she is content to respond superficially and only mention trivial detail. As soon as I stray into a domain that is too sensitive, words fail her and she quickly shifts to something inconsequential. I then get the impression that if she took her thoughts to a conclusion, she would melt. In spite of all that, her strength sometimes surprised me.

I telephoned her shortly after I was contacted for the first time by the Prime Minister's Office. My interlocutor had asked me to try to obtain information from my mother to bolster my file.

'Mum, Marianne[29] mentioned the beautiful jewels your mother used to wear. She told me that you were rich.'

---

29 My great-aunt, the wife of Ernst, brother of Kaethe, my grandmother.

'Beautiful jewels...? How could my mother have had any...? From Sophie Schnurmann... She was a very rich woman, Monica.'

'And who was this Sophie Schnurmann?'

'She was Fritz's mother.'

'Who was Fritz?'

'My father...'

'Mum, so Sophie Schnurmann was your grandmother!'

'Yes... I think that's right.'

'So it was your family! Your family was the rich one!'

'Yes, Monica. We had a beautiful, spacious house, and Sophie Schnurmann lived there with us.'

'Do you remember the jewels?'

'I've been searching my memory for years for my mother's face. It always eludes me. I can remember my father, but my mother...'

'But you were more than ten years old when she died, weren't you?'

'Monica, doesn't the cold get at you in Paris?'

I know her abrupt change of subject was only a reflex action to protect herself from danger.

The following week, I resumed the conversation about the jewels with her. She once again avoided any direct allusion to her mother; she nevertheless recounted that when they reached the Gare de l'Est in Paris in 1938, she, Edith, was holding a doll in one hand and a bag full of jewels in the other; she had carried them as if they were playthings for her doll.

My mother is not full of hate. On the contrary, she is a good, generous woman. She has taught us to look generously upon those who are in need or who are distressed. Nonetheless, she is not particularly sympathetic when it is a matter of psychological suffering. Similarly, she refuses to be affected by the sight of physical injuries. She can even at times seem very hard. When I was small and hurt myself, she might go into fits of laughter and in the end I stopped showing her my cuts because her reaction would upset me. I found the way to the chemists and went by myself to get a cure. If the knock were benign, I'd treat myself, even though I couldn't stand the sight of blood: I would sometimes faint. And when the seriousness of my condition meant I had to go to hospital, my mother never took me, because she couldn't bear to.

13

The Lie Tactic

In his letter of 12 July 2001, the chairman of L'Oréal, Mr Owen-Jones wrote that the Haarfarben und Parfümerien GmbH Company, the German subsidiary of L'Oréal, 'bought the adjacent land and built an office block on the terrain'. As he didn't specify what the land adjacent to Wendstrasse 19 was, I immediately thought of Wendstrasse 17. Now Wendstrasse 19 is on the corner of Wendstrasse and Kaiserallee[30].

The land to which Owen-Jones refers is in fact situated at Kaiserallee 18 and backs onto Wendstrasse 19. My misunderstanding sent my research along a path I would certainly not have followed otherwise. It enabled me to make a fantastic discovery. Luck was on my side.

My mistake led me to discover what happened at number 17. I called Mr Müller at the land registry in Karlruhe. I asked him who owned Wendstrasse 17. He replied: 'A company by the name of Ensa.'
'What does it do?'
'*A priori* it's a perfumery.'
'When did it buy Wendstrasse 17?'
'In 1951.'

---

30 The sketch on p 68 merely indicates the position of the lots and doesn't attempt to represent the real scale.

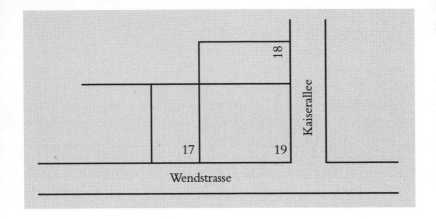

This company's business and the date of the sale in 1951 made me prick up my ears. 'Mr Müller, can you see who signed the bill of sale on behalf of Ensa?' I asked.

'A Mr Tondu.'

'André Tondu?'

'Yes.'

It was the same person who had bought Wendstrasse 19! He was the person mandated by Haarfarben und Parfümerien, alias L'Oréal, to buy our house at Wendstrasse 19 in 1954. André Tondu… His name appeared on the bill of sale agreed between the Badischer Gemeinde Versicherung Verband (BGV), who appropriated our house in 1938, and L'Oréal.

'Does one company sometimes hide behind another in order not to appear in public?' I asked ingenuously.

'Yes, it's called a front company.'

'I have the feeling that L'Oréal is hiding behind Ensa.'

'It could well be. Mention it to your lawyer.'

'One last thing, in relation to the date of purchase: can you find out if they expressed an interest in this lot before 1951?'

I asked the question because I'd noticed that in the 1954 bill of sale, in which the BGV ceded Wendstrasse 19 to L'Oréal, it was noted that Mr André Tondu had been already designated in 1953 to carry out the purchase.

'I'll have a look. Call me back this afternoon.'

I called him as agreed.

'Yes, something did happen in February 1949.'

'What?'

He didn't reply. I persisted: 'Mr Müller, I'm sure it was L'Oréal that bought Wendstrasse 17. I'll have to consult with my lawyer to see how I can prove it. Meanwhile, if this bill of sale relates to my property at number 19, you have the right to make me a copy, don't you?'

'I'll send you one right away.'

I telephoned my lawyer to tell him of my discovery. He asked me to research Ensa Ltd. So I contacted the company registry in Karlsruhe and asked for information on that company, as well as on L'Oréal and Haarfarben und Parfümerien GmbH.

A few days later, an official called me, rather panic-stricken: 'I started to look out the documents you requested. It's impossible to send you all this, there is just too much. What's more, it will cost you a fortune…'

I joked, to try to calm her down, and said I didn't want to cause her any problems. I then explained why these documents were so important for me. She passed me on to her boss to whom I repeated my story. We reached a compromise: she would send me the documents from the 1940s and the beginning of the 1950s; I would phone her if I needed any more.

The documents I received contained a wealth of information: L'Oréal's address was the same as Ensa's, Wendstrasse 17, and the two companies were managed by the same man, André Tondu. But I felt I was a long way from finding out the whole truth. The future would not belie my hunch.

In this same month of August, the Versorgung des Bundes und der Länder, the present owners of Wendstrasse 19 after buying it from L'Oréal in 1991, also replied to our letter sent in June: they considered they weren't subject to our claims. In any case, the letter refrained from stating that the property didn't belong to us and referred us back to the seller: L'Oréal, as it turned out.

Autumn came and the rehearsals of *Rigoletto* began at such a hectic pace I hardly had time to think about anything but work. It was then I received details of the famous irrefutable evidence mentioned by L'Oréal's CEO. In fact, it was the document I had already received from the BGV insurance company where it says the dispute was settled in 1951 via a Jewish organization. My great-uncle Karl Rosenfelder had apparently signed this agreement, something BGV had already stated, without being able to supply evidence of his signature.

After the war, a court case was begun against BGV, accused of having stolen property owned by Jews. My mother hadn't even been informed. The signature appearing on the 1938 bill of sale of our house to BGV was that of a certain Luise Dürr. This woman, who was totally unknown to my family, disposed of the Rosenfelders' property by virtue of a power of attorney my grandfather had granted her under constraint in order to allow his wife (my grandmother), daughter (my mother) and mother-in-law to leave Germany and join him in Paris. Nonetheless, as the signature of my grandmother Kaethe didn't appear on the 1938 bill of sale, the court had supported the central indictment: BGV had well and truly stolen our property.

I had the feeling there had been an unpleasant invasion of the intimacy of our family: I was ill again. I felt sullied, couldn't think any more and spent hours in the bath. I did not understand how some people could be in possession of these documents when we, the individuals most affected, had only just discovered their existence. I later found out that they were not held in an archive that was open to the public.

I spent a week digesting this evidence. This time I said nothing to my mother; I wanted to spare her this latest insult. When I was in a state to think once more, I tried to gather together all the pieces of the puzzle: I had to get to grips with L'Oréal's tactics. Why were they acting as if they didn't know when it had been demonstrated that the property had been in the possession of the Nazis?

The tactic of sheltering behind a lie is well known. Didn't *Maître* Zaoui himself speak of this tactic during the Touvier trial when he quoted the remarks of a man called Kramer who was being tried for the responsibilities he held in an extermination camp? To the question 'What was the purpose of the gas chambers?' the Nazi criminal had replied: 'I don't know.'[31]

An irony of fate, at that very moment, the History Channel was broadcasting images from the Barbie trial[32]. *Maître* Zaoui pleads there in the name of the Jews who suffered the atrocities inflicted by their Nazi executioner. To quote him: 'Our dead cry out to us: Never forget! Never! Never!'

Yes, *Maître*, our dead cry out those words to us.

---

31 *Maître* Zaoui was quoting from an extract from the legal reports of a trial of camp leaders and their aides. This trial took place in Frankfurt from 1963 to 1965.
32 The Klaus Barbie trial was held from 11 May to 4 July 1987.

14

The Giant Octopus

L'Oréal is a large multinational conglomerate comprising a multitude of brands such as:

L'Oréal de Paris: Elsève, Elnett, Studioline, Préférence, Excellence, Open Color, Feria, Plénitude, L'Oréal Perfection;

Garnier: Fructis, Ultra Doux, Nutrisse, Lumia, Belle Color, Synergie, Ambre Solaire;

Maybelline New York: Jade, Gemey, Ylang, Colorama;

Softsheen-Carson;

Club des Créateurs de Beauté: Agnès B., Corinne Cobson, Jean-Marc Maniatis, Marina Marinof, Michel Klein, Tan Giudicelli;

Dop, Mixa, Narta, Obao, La Roche-Posay, Vichy.

The following luxury products catch one's eye:

Lancôme, Biotherm, Helena Rubinstein, Kiehl's, Shu Uemura;

Giorgio Armani, Cacharel, Ralph Lauren, Guy Laroche, Paloma Picasso.

And in pharmaceuticals, there is the *Sanofi-Synthélabo* group, controlled by L'Oréal and Total Fina Elf [33].

Given the advertising clout that all these brands represent, it is easy to imagine the reserves of energy, and much besides, that newspapers must deploy in order to dare to publish stories like ours.

---

33 In 2005 the *Sanofi-Synthelabo* group became the *Sanofi-Aventis* group.

The capital structure of L'Oréal was as follows in 2003[34]:

> 53.70 per cent of L'Oréal's capital belongs to *Gesparal*. Mme Bettencourt and her family hold 51 per cent of the shares in *Gesparal*[35], and *Nestlé* 49 per cent.
>
> 46.30 per cent of L'Oréal capital is publicly held.

Other information[36]:

> The chief executive is Lindsay Owen-Jones; the vice-chair of the Board of Directors is Jean-Pierre Meyers[37].
>
> The directors include: Liliane Bettencourt, Françoise Bettencourt-Meyers, and François Dalle.

In the documentation sent by the Karlsruhe business registry, one can see that the shareholders of L'Oréal Deutschland – previously called Haarfarben und Parfümerien GmbH – both of French nationality, shared the capital as follows in 1931 when the enterprise was created, and then when it was transferred to Karlsruhe:

> Eugène Bricout held 39,000 German marks;
>
> André Tondu held 1,000 German marks.

This distribution of capital remained almost unchanged up to Eugène Schueller's death in August 1957. One wonders why Liliane Bettencourt took over Eugène Bricout's shares without any sale being noted in the business registry, at least in the documents I've been sent.

Thus, in March 1958, the capital of Haarfarben und Parfümerien[38] was distributed among the following shareholders:

---

34 This information is supplied on the L'Oréal Internet site.

35 The person who holds 51 per cent of the capital of a firm wields total power within the board of directors.

36 Also supplied on the L'Oréal Internet site.

37 In April 2006 Jean Paul Agon became the CEO of L'Oréal and Lindsay Owen-Jones the non-executive chair of the board of L'Oréal.

38 Reminder: 'Colouring for hair and perfumes'.

Mr Eugène Bricout,	
resident in the region of the Seine[39]	57,000 DM
Mr André Tondu,	
resident Wendstrasse 17, Karlsruhe	1,500 DM
Mr Auguste Huntzinger,	
resident region of the Seine	500 DM
Mr Gaston Lechène,	
resident region of the Seine	500 DM
Mr Marcel Jussier,	
resident region of the Seine	500 DM

But Eugène Bricout disappeared in June 1959. The capital was then distributed between:

Mrs André Bettencourt,	80,000 + 16,000 =
née Liliane Schueller, resident	96,000 DM
Neuilly-sur-Seine	
Mr André Tondu, Karlsruhe	2,500 DM
Mr Auguste Huntzinger, Seine	500 DM
Mr Gaston Lechène, Seine	500 DM
Mr Marcel Jussier, Seine	500 DM

They were all represented, with the exception of Mr Tondu, by one Henri Fèbvre, a lawyer, resident 4 rue Rodin in Paris. All this was set out and broadcast on L'Oréal headed notepaper from…1950. Besides, Henri Fèbvre was one of Eugène Schueller's seven collaborators, with whom the latter and his daughter held shares in L'Oréal, Schueller and Liliane Bettencourt being the majority shareholders[40].

And in 1961, the date when L'Oréal *officially* appeared in the Haarfarben und Parfümerien portfolio, the group is entered as a minority shareholder, replacing the minority shareholders of 1959:

---

39 His address is explicitly mentioned as are those of all the other shareholders living in France.
40 Bruno Abescat, *La saga des Bettencourt*, op.cit., p. 186.

L'Oréal SA, Paris	1,1410,000 DM
Mr Henri Fèbvre, Paris	50,000 DM
Mrs André Bettencourt, Paris	80,000 DM[41]

In 1962 Orinter became the firm with majority shareholding in Haarfarben und Parfümerien. And the distribution of holdings in 1965 was as follows:

Orinter SA Paris	3,760,000 DM
Mrs Bettencourt, Neuilly-sur-Seine	107,000 DM
Mr Henri Fèbvre, Paris	133,000 DM

The figures continue to grow to 1968, but there was no change in the shareholders. And new minority shareholders appeared in 1969:

Orinter SA, Paris	9,964,000 DM
Mrs Bettencourt, Neuilly-sur-Seine	485,000 DM
Mr Dalle, Neuilly-sur-Seine	42,000 DM
Mr Lefèbvre, Brussels	42,000 DM
Mr Henri Fèbvre, Paris	3,000 DM

The following year, L'Oréal replaced Orinter, while the other shareholders remained the same.

This somewhat onerous list of names and figures shows that Mrs Bettencourt appears before 1961. Now, Mr Owen-Jones stated that L'Oréal was not involved in this company prior to 1961. However, we should recall that L'Oréal's first name was 'French company for harmless hair dyes', very similar to Haarfarben und Parfümerien's name – 'Colouring for hair and perfumes' – and one can hardly believe Liliane Bettencourt held shares in a German company which had the same market aims as L'Oréal (perfumes and cosmetics), and that the French company was never involved. Mr Owen-Jones can make all the chronological caveats he likes; I will continue to think he travesties the truth.

---

41 Documents from the Karlsruhe town hall.

I should also add that the fact that French citizens like Eugène Schueller and André Tondu went on to found a company in Germany in the 1930s is not exactly reassuring. If they hadn't been somewhat in accord with the ideas being propounded by the Nazi regime, I doubt that the enterprise known as L'Oréal could have made much headway in Berlin. Moreover, Eugène Schueller paid a visit to the German Embassy 18 March 1942. I have, from the Frydman brothers, the copy of a document from the German Embassy. It is a report listing the people received at the embassy that day and the reasons for their visit. It records how Schueller had come to proclaim his loyalty to Hitler[42].

---

42 This information is also quoted by Michel Bar-Zohar, op.cit., pp. 57-58.

15

De-Nazification?

I kept on putting the puzzle together by looking for new pieces. I directed my research at another passage in one of Mr Owen-Jones's letters: 'In 1954 […], the insurance company ceded the empty land (as the building was destroyed during the war) to Haarfarben und Parfümerien GmbH, the German subsidiary of L'Oréal.' This isn't totally correct: our house, bombed during the war, was on this land. What state was it in? We weren't there at the time to see for ourselves.

The reconstruction of Germany was financed by different economic aid plans, the best known of which is America's Marshall Plan. These plans allowed new buildings to be erected to replace those destroyed by bombing. It wouldn't be a total nonsense to imagine that L'Oréal could have benefited from such aid to build on the lot they had just purchased.

I needed the help of specialists to throw light on this and finally found them at the German Institute for History in Paris. I was given the names of three researchers, and one of them rang me a few days later. After hearing my story, he gave me some clues to help me in my research. Thanks to his advice, I learned that L'Oréal's financial guarantor had been the town of Karlsruhe itself and that the construction of the new building was financed by the Rheine Bank am Main. Then he advised me to contact one of his colleagues who specialized in this area. The latter gave me an appointment.

I took part of the already considerable pile of documents I had assembled so far to this meeting. My interlocutor, like others before him, was taken aback; once he'd got over his amazement, he informed me of some very pertinent facts: immediately after the war, the town of Karlsruhe was put under French aegis before being handed over to the United States. It was this Allied supervision that set in motion the rebuilding of the town. The financing came from different bodies, including banks, and everything was under the baton of a certain Hermann J. Abs. This individual, although responsible for the looting perpetrated by the Nazi regime[43], had managed to become the spokesman for the Allies in relation to the *return* of their property to the Jews. Moreover, he was director of the Deutsche Bank, until in the 1970s protests were voiced in Germany against the fact that so prominent an ex-Nazi occupied such an important post. He was called upon to resign and did so. Finally, the regional name for the Deutsche Bank was at the time…Rheine Bank am Main, and it was thus this same Hermann J. Abs who oversaw the bank which financed the construction of the L'Oréal building.

My adviser also explained to me that if the BGV insurance company had been able to take over a building as important as ours in 1938, it could only have been because its leaders at the time were affiliated to the Nazi Party; it was the necessary 'open sesame' for operations of that size. But, after the war, the game went into reverse for the majority of ex-Nazis: in order to have any hopes of continuing their work, they had to emerge immaculate from the so-called de-nazification tribunals. If they were found guilty, they lost part of their civil rights, and that could be a source of great future difficulties. Thus, a number of these ex-Nazis found a token Jew or member of the Resistance to give evidence in their favour so they would be acquitted. According to this expert, I was in my rights to demand to see the file on the de-nazification of those in charge of BGV.

I was very moved by the generosity shown towards me by the researchers at the German Institute for History. As I lived through those moments of my life, meeting people of this calibre reminded me that good people do also exist. I have fortunately met many more, and they have been

---

43 See Eberhard Czichon, *Deutsche Bank Macht Politik. Fascismus, Krieg und Bundesrepublik*, PapyRossa Verlag, 2001, p. 123.

a great source of comfort. Following the advice of these researchers, I started to look for the documentation on the de-nazification of the staff at BGV. To obtain this kind of document, one has to have been a victim of the Nazis or belong to the family of a victim. It was on this basis that I gained access.

Erwin Brunner, the managing director of BGV, was definitely a member of the Nazi Party when the insurance company took over our house in 1938. He even belonged to the SA[44]. I should point out that the SA's headquarters in Karlsruhe was based in a house that had belonged to Jews – the Weils, friends of our family – and it was right opposite…Wendstrasse 19.

At the end of the war, the priority for some Nazis wasn't so much to do good business as to *prove* that they had never been Nazis. In short, it was essential to procure a whitewash: when questioned, the verbatim reports of which are in his de-nazification file, Mr Erwin Brunner stated that he 'became a Nazi and a member of the SA in order to help the Jews'. There's always a good reason for everything!

It is easy to see that his company, the BGV, urgently needed to offload a property taken from Jews, namely our townhouse. L'Oréal, through Haarfarben und Parfümerien, was a providential purchaser. The image of this company that arrived in Karlsruhe with the Allies who had fought the Nazis was perfect. It was only much later that it became public knowledge that L'Oréal had given important posts to a number of enforcers of Nazi policies or *cagoulards* like Jacques Corrèze.

I received documents from the Karlsruhe business registry attesting to the fact that Mr André Tondu worked on behalf of L'Oréal at Wendstrasse 17. I recalled that this gentleman figures first, as director-general of Ensa in the bill of sale which gave it ownership of Wendstrasse 17 in 1951, then as the representative of L'Oréal in the 1954 bill of sale of Wendstrasse 19 from BGV to L'Oréal.

A few days later, my lawyer telephoned me: 'Mrs Waitzfelder, I am rereading the documents from the business registry that you brought me,

---

44 *Sturmabteilung* – storm-troopers: the Nazi Party's armed militia, which was subsequently replaced by the SS (Schutzstaffel – protection group).

and I have just come across something that is quite incredible. Do you remember what you found on the Internet site for L'Oréal Deutschland?'

We had completely forgotten this document. It was among those I'd given him at our first meeting.

'Just listen,' he continued, 'to what they write on the presentation on the site under the rubric of "history": "*Quite the first stone of this unparalleled success was laid in 1930 in Berlin by André Tondu, when Eugène Schueller, the founder of the French firm, mandated him to conquer the German hairdressing market. The first steps taken by Haarfarben und Parfümerien GmbH were not easy. Of course, the first dyes were quickly accepted by the market, but the Berlin base was destroyed in the war and, in 1945, a new factory was to be built in Karlsruhe."'*

What did they think we were? Backward? The chief executive of L'Oréal didn't even know what his own company's website said about its creation in Germany! André Tondu had never worked for L'Oréal? L'Oréal never had connections with Wendstrasse 17? Somewhat hard to believe!

What was becoming clearer and clearer was the goal of L'Oréal's real-estate operations in Karlsruhe: the creation of a vast holding in a well-to-do part of town. They would erect a big building (where our house was) on the biggest lot, Wendstrasse 19, situated on the corner of Wendstrasse and Kaiserallee 18, and the two adjoining lots – Wendstrasse 17 and Kaiserallee 18 – would be used as annexes, car park, garden… But the centrepiece of this complex remained Wendstrasse 19; without the latter, the whole operation would have been impossible.

Maître Korman then sent me to a court bailiff. The latter drew up a statement to attest to the existence of the information posted on the Internet by L'Oréal and of its continued link with André Tondu[45].

We resumed our scrutiny of the bill of sale of Wendstrasse 17 by Ensa. Number 17 was the object of a strange two-stage purchase: a first bill of purchase signed in February 1949 was followed bizarrely by a second confirming the first. The second bill was signed in October 1951 and was published in the property register on 5 November 1951: that is, the *very*

45 See Appendix 14.

day when BGV was reaching its so-called agreement with a Jewish organization in relation to Wendstrasse 19[46]. It was henceforth clear that L'Oréal's purchase of number 17 (via the front company Ensa) was closely linked to the forthcoming purchase of number 19. Contrary to what L'Oréal tried to make us believe, it was far from 'discovering' Wendstrasse 19 in 1954. The company had set its sights on the plot at least in 1948 but couldn't buy it before this date because the property was still subject to Allied military government law. André Tondu for L'Oréal in Germany, representing Eugène Schueller, then applied a practice that is quite usual in the world of business: discretion, nay, dissimulation – by making no public display of interest in Wendstrasse 19. The purchase of the different lots was to be achieved via different companies.

Maître Korman now told me that this was more than presumption on our part...

---

46 See Appendices 7 and 8.

16

My Father

Before the war, my father was a medical student in Heidelberg. With his blond hair and blue eyes, he was like the majority of his fellow German citizens, but his origins prevented him from continuing with his studies. He had a friend, Wolfgang, whose father was a shipbuilder. When Wolfgang saw the reprisals meted out against Jews on *Kristallnacht*[47], he rushed his friend on board one of his father's ships; this ship was bound for Brazil.

Before he had barely recovered from the shock caused by this brutal uprooting, my father left for Amazonia to work for a company that dealt in precious stones. He had to work as quickly as possible and earn enough to pay for his own needs. He also had to pay a ransom for his parents who were still in Germany: he had to pay this money to the German Consulate each month in order to safeguard their lives.

Years later, my father would tell me of the cruel, humiliating game to which his father fell victim. Like other old Jews, he was forced to spend hours kneeling in frozen streets, in the middle of winter, his torso naked and arms crossed; anyone who was unfortunate enough to lower their arms was immediately killed. And many were.

---

47 After an attack perpetrated by a Jew on the German Embassy in Paris and the death of the Embassy attaché von Rath, the German Minister for Propaganda, Joseph Goebbels, denounced ' a Jewish conspiracy' against Germany and unleashed a vast pogrom. Over the night of 9 and 10 November 1938, SA storm troopers, the SS and the Hitler Youth pillaged and smashed up thousands of shops and burned a hundred synagogues. Almost a hundred people were killed.

My father was a nervous man and perpetually on the move. He only calmed down when we went to the country house in Itaipava. He needed to be close to the forest; that contact with nature made him another person. And that was when he spoke to us of important matters.

He would often to talk to me about such things when we returned from a walk at twilight and took a dirt track we knew by heart and which could lead us home with our eyes closed. It was on this track that he told me that my Rosenfelder grandparents had died because of the Nazis and that my grandmother had died in a concentration camp (I'm not sure he mentioned the name of the camp). I would usually harass him with questions, but now I asked none. I didn't ask him what a concentration camp was, what my grandparents' names were or in what circumstances they died. I was perhaps too young to do so. I was perhaps aware that what he had just told me was the cause of my mother's sorrow. I too was perhaps already suffering from this. I knew nothing. And my father, in response to my silence, didn't pursue the subject.

Nevertheless, I remember that day as if it were yesterday. We started our return as the sky regaled us with the flamboyant spectacle of a Brazilian twilight. Here, in France, the colours are different at dusk: it is a palette of blue, bluish-grey with an occasional hint of orange that the eye retains. There, orange and fiery red predominate but are gradually absorbed by black after an orangey-brown phase.

Night had almost fallen when we suddenly heard a noise. We stopped and saw a peasant hitting a snake with a stick that kept breaking at every blow. There was nothing unusual about killing snakes in Itaipava. Serpents abounded, and even we children would do the same if they represented a danger to life; otherwise everyone went their respective way.

But this reptile was incredibly long, exceptionally big. It was more than two metres long with a bodily circumference of around twenty centimetres. My father took off his jacket, signalled to me to keep away while he lent the peasant a hand. It took the two men a long time to get the better of the huge snake. They finally crushed its head with the help of a big stone. Then they exchanged a few words along the lines of 'The brute put up a good fight' and 'Thanks for your help' before my father picked up his jacket, and we resumed our walk.

It was now pitch dark, but we hadn't switched our torches on. We walked on silently until he said: 'You won't tell anyone what you saw this evening, will you?'

'Why?'

'Because people won't believe you. They'll say you're spinning a tall story, and I don't want people to think of you as a liar. It will be a secret between us.'

I have always kept that nocturnal scene to myself, when I saw my father level that huge snake which today reminds me of Nazism. Later in life, I mentioned the incident to him, probably because I wanted to reassure myself it wasn't a nightmare. He was surprised that I remembered, and I was happy then to have that secret I could share with my father.

To this day, I have never spoken about it to anyone. There is no way I would want to be thought of as a spinner of tall stories.

17

Hell is Other People

L'Oréal maintains it bears no responsibility for the robbery; one should take it further back to the BGV insurance company. Despite the tragic events of which the robbery is part, I cannot help feeling it's like children bickering: 'Sir, 'snot me, it's him!'

My mother prefers to quote Sartre: 'Hell is other people.'

My mother, of whose existence L'Oréal pretended to be unaware at the time it was purchasing Wendstrasse 19… I think it's impossible they didn't know she was alive. Mr. Owen-Jones wrote on 12 July 2001, as part of his irrefutable evidence, that he only learned of my mother's existence when he read our letter of 18 June 2001. I don't believe this statement for one minute. When you buy a property, Mr. Owen-Jones, don't you check who the owner is? There must be a very poor information-flow in your enterprise indeed if your predecessors never told you where this property came from: even more so, dear sir, given that you must have known that Wendstrasse 19 was the biggest L'Oréal head office in Europe after Paris.

My mother has always kept her German nationality. From her arrival in Brazil in December 1946, she has regularly gone to the German Consulate in Rio to get her passport renewed. Moreover, as she was a minor at that time, the Jewish institutions responsible for her had supervised her itinerary and made sure she arrived safely at her Uncle Ernst's in Sao Paolo. The latter's address was consequently known, and she lived there until she married in October 1951. Additionally, after she'd left there, there was always someone living at the address that knew how to find her. In order to marry, my mother had to get a certificate of her civil status from the town hall of the municipality where she was born. The Karlsruhe public administration was then perfectly aware of her existence since her certificate of birth[48] is not followed by any death certificate, unlike her mother Kaethe's, which mentions '*deceased at Auschwitz, 27 September 1942*'. For anyone who took the trouble, my mother wasn't difficult to track down. Mr. Müller has moreover informed me that the Karlsruhe civil registry was in the same building as the land registry – and on the same floor as well!

L'Oréal and BGV pretend they were unaware of the existence of survivors among those with a claim on the house. The forgetfulness of these companies did not only relate to my mother but also extended to another survivor: my great-uncle Karl. Yet, who mentioned Karl Rosenfelder's name after the war as a supposed signatory to the 1951 agreement, if it wasn't first BGV and then L'Oréal? These companies knew there was at least one survivor since they both mentioned him.

I have equally wondered hard about the JRSO, the Jewish organization that concluded that 'agreement' with BGV. That a Jewish organization should have concerned itself with a stolen property that *a priori* had no heirs at the end of the war is fine – such was its role. But I was really astonished that *a posteriori* it had let the property fall into hands other than those of its living owners. How on earth could it have concluded an agreement detrimental to the interests of those who had the rights to the property? Did it have no other solution or did it yield to pressure?

At night I often woke up and resumed my reading. It was in the course of one of these bouts of insomnia that I reread this famous 'agreement' between BGV and the JRSO. As I often did, I looked at the German original and the French translation side by side: I felt the need to experience two different readings of the same document at the same time.

---

48 See Appendix 2.

And suddenly, after rereading the third clause of the 'agreement' of 5 November 1951, I understood its significance and implications: '*The JRSO undertakes, inasmuch as the defendant (the BGV) acts in conformity with the instructions from the JRSO, to compensate the defendant to a maximum of 5,000 DM if a situation arises where those with a priority right make themselves known and validly undermine the defendant's position.*'

Clearly, this clause means that if those enjoying ownership rights come forward, the JRSO must reimburse the insurance company to the sum of 5,000 DM: the agreement is annulled and those with ownership rights regain these legitimate rights at the expense of the robber, the BGV[49].

It all started to get much clearer in my head! Here before my eyes was the reason why they had refused to supply us with documentation from the title deeds that we had requested from Karlsruhe: these papers would have allowed us to annul this 'agreement' by establishing that we had the right of ownership of our property.

A shiver ran down my spine.

For the first time, I understood why we had gone through so many difficult years and why they had told my mother she was mad when she had repeatedly tried to ensure her rights prevailed before I even got involved. There was in effect a good reason to go mad in the face of such attitudes, and I reckoned that, all in all, my mother had stood up to them remarkably well.

By dint of hearing it repeated so often that she was imagining things, she had sometimes doubted the truth of her own suffering to the point of wondering whether the pain she experienced was really legitimate. How could she mourn for her own history if it weren't true? But at the same time, how could she resign herself to the fact it was untrue when she was haunted by so many memories?

All this wore down my mother tremendously. For years, her memories couldn't be connected to any reality whatsoever; the trauma of the Shoah prevented any individual healing, and mourning couldn't have its effect for over more than fifty years. Thus, L'Oréal had denied a whole family that

---

49 See Appendix 8.

had lived through this terrible experience the right to mourn those sombre years. And today, by continuing to lie, L'Oréal scorned our suffering and forced us to relive everything again. By denying what they'd done, they were very close to telling us we had invented everything.

That is why I bear such a grudge against L'Oréal, because they took everything from us. Our history as well as our home.

18
Like Father, Like Son-in-Law!

In 1991 Jean Frydman, an important Jewish businessman, entered into conflict with François Dalle, L'Oréal's chief executive at the time with whom he had enjoyed friendship and a business relationship in a film production company they had founded together[50]. Jean Frydman challenged his exclusion from the board of directors that was decided at a meeting in his absence[51]. He contested the decision in court, and François Dalle was subsequently found guilty of 'deception, misrepresentation and racial discrimination'[52]. As a result of this, with the help of his brother David, Jean Frydman began to investigate L'Oréal's past and discovered the dubious connections that linked Eugène Schueller, its founder, and other directors of the company with the Vichy government.

I devoted time to tracking down the whereabouts of the Frydman brothers. I rang David Frydman's company only to learn that he had died. Nonetheless, I set up a meeting with Jean-Pierre Pelletier, who supported Jean Frydman in the case that brought them into conflict with L'Oréal. Mr Pelletier gave me the warmest of welcomes. He listened carefully and looked

---

50 The Panavision Company – 75 per cent of its capital was from L'Oréal, the remaining 25 per cent from Jean Frydman, in the form of their film list.

51 For more information on this, see Michel Bar-Zohar, op. cit.

52 *Le Monde*, 7 March 2002, reports: 'François Dalle was found guilty in 1991 of 'deception, misrepresentation and racial discrimination', but the charge was dismissed on 4 December 1992 after an out-of-court settlement was reached with Jean Frydman.

at the documents I'd brought before he explained to me the stage they had reached in their legal action. He also gave me some very useful advice.

When I mentioned my surprise at the fact that everyone who gravitated around L'Oréal hid the truth, he responded that the Frydman brothers had met the same problem; such had always been the case when anyone took on L'Oréal.

Jean-Pierre Pelletier, a really kind, understanding man, sent me two books written by David and Jean Frydman entitled *L'Affaire Bettencourt* and *Pour la mémoire*[53].

These two books bring together documents attesting to the relationship between André Bettencourt, Eugène Schueller, leading management of L'Oréal and the Nazis.

Far from being the resistance fighter he always pretended to be, André Bettencourt − Schueller's son-in-law − was a zealous collaborator. From 1941 he wrote for a journal, *La Terre française*, which published, among other things, the speeches of Pétain, Darlan and Laval. This magazine was the personal responsibility of von Ribbentrop within the framework of the German propaganda machine and was connected to the French section of the *Propagandastaffel*. The latter was declared a Nazi criminal organization in the course of the Nuremberg trials.

At least seventy-one articles in this journal advocating hatred of the Jews carry the by-line of future minister, André Bettencourt. The strongly anti-Semitic content of these articles all made me feel sick:

'Jews, those hypocritical Pharisees can hope no more. It is all over for them, they have no faith. They carry within themselves no possibility of rectification. Their race is eternally soiled by the blood of the just. They will be damned, everyone of them [...] The Jews of today, not in race but in thought, will be and are already vomit.'[54]

---

53 Both these books were self-published in 2002 and were never published commercially.
54 *La Terre française* 24, 12 April 1941, 'Easter Bells'.

'One day, thirty years later, the Jews imagined nevertheless they were going to win. They had managed to lay their hands on Jesus and had crucified him. Rubbing their hand together, they proclaimed: may his blood spill on us and on our children. You know moreover the way in which it was spilt and continues to spill. The teachings in the eternal book must be fulfilled.'[55]

Freemasons were not spared either. André Bettencourt harboured a particularly virulent hostility towards them:

'Pimps (one could call them such since they are the real criminals, the real supporters of the rotten regime) [...] still carry out the will of the lodges, systematically loot, either from disability, or dishonesty, the coffers of France.'[56]

'Marshal Pétain has given us three keywords 'Work, Family, Fatherland'. We have already erased from the façades of our town halls the triple device of Masonic liberalism.'[57]

The above extracts were not written by a junior or peripheral contributor. André Bettencourt was the main editor of *La Terre française*, its most influential political collaborator. His responsibility for the messages of hate he distilled for the benefit of this journal is thus that much weightier.

The chapter in Jean and David Frydman's book dedicated to Mr Bettencourt's prose during the Occupation concludes on this note:

We have also showed to what extent his articles correlate with some of the most tragic periods of collaboration, particularly successive stages in the persecution of Jews and freemasons. At the time when André Bettencourt was publishing his editorials, the psychological preparation for genocides had been put in place. The Wannsee conference, in the course of which the total extermination of the Jews was decided, took place three weeks after the publication of his prophetic article of 20 December 1941, its title so pregnant with

---

55 *La Terre française* 60, 20 December 1941, 'Christmas, Star of Hope'.
56 *La Terre française* 33, 14 June 1941, 'Pimps'.
57 *La Terre française* 42, 16 August 1941, 'The Charter for Youth'.

meaning: 'Christmas, Star of Hope'. A correlation confirming, if this was necessary, that his articles were not written as random reflections but were perfectly synchronized with the orders of the Nazi authorities as conveyed by certain journals, like *La Terre française* or *L'Élan*.[58]

'Should it be a duty to inform?' André Bettencourt also wrote. 'Yes, inasmuch as this really helps the collectivity[…] Young people must be the Marshal's agents in every village, that is to say the police of the Revolution.'[59]

My mother has told me how quickly she had to leave 6 rue des Saussaies to flee to unoccupied territory after Kaethe (her mother), Emma (her maternal grandmother) and she herself were informed on. Moreover, I've never found out who betrayed them.

In the aftermath of the war, the man knew how to cover up his past. Jacques Baynac notes, in *Les Secrets de l'affaire Jean Moulin. Archives inédites sur la Résistance*: 'In the summer of 1944, Bettencourt will be able, thanks to him (the Resistance fighter Pierre de Bénouville) and Mitterand, to spend a little over a month in Geneva, thus cheaply acquiring a certificate as a member of the Resistance that he really needed in order to cover up his previous activities which were pro-Pétain or worse.'[60]

In 1947 André Bettencourt succeeded his father as chair of the Council for the Lillebonne district in Seine-Maritime. In 1951 he became a deputy for the same province. From 1954 to 1972, he went from being Secretary to the Council of Ministers, to Secretary of State for Transport, then Foreign Affairs and Minister for Telecommunications, then Industry, finally Minister with special responsibilities for the environment, and then for Foreign Affairs. The past finally caught up with André Bettencourt, and he had to resign in 1994 from the company and put a definitive end to his political career.

58 *L'Affaire Bettencourt*, op cit.
59 *La Terre française* 50, 11 October 1941.
60 Jacques Baynac, *Les Secrets de l'affaire Jean Moulin. Archives inédites sur la Résistance*, Paris, Le Seuil, 1998.

Schueller was fanatically anti–Semitic, anti–Freemason, Fascist and the financer of La Cagoule. André Bettencourt met him in 1938. Both evidently shared a range of ideas. In issue 58 of *La Terre française*, one reads from the pen of André Bettencourt:

'The hope of youth: to be an employer [...] my plucky young lad! I gave him a remarkable book to read by my friend, M.E. Schueller, entitled *La Révolution de l'Economie*. This is a book that all company directors of today and tomorrow should read. It is a young book par excellence...'

On 18 March 1942, Eugène Schueller proclaimed his loyalty to Hitler. After the liberation of France, he got a miraculous whitewash thanks to a man who put all his energy into avoiding national disgrace and prison. This man, who became his son–in–law in 1950, was none other than André Bettencourt. He provided shelter and protection in the heart of L'Oréal to his father–in–law and to a large number of *cagoulards* and the worst adepts of collaboration.

The past resurfaced in the 1990s with the Frydman case. In June 2000, the 'Association of Parisian Chemists for Memory', backed by a range of distinguished individuals, took the decision to change the name of the 'Eugène Schueller' lecture theatre, as did the 1961 class at the National Higher Institute for Chemistry, in order to underline their refusal to associate the school with the name of a fascist.

Jean Frydman also crossed swords with Jacques Corrèze, another old acquaintance of Eugène Schueller. The then chair of Cosmair, the US branch of L'Oréal, played a key role in excluding Jean Frydman from the board of directors in 1989. It should be recalled that before the war Jacques Corrèze was one of the thugs in La Cagoule, the pro–Hitler terrorist organization that often met at the L'Oréal headquarters on the rue Royale, and for which Eugène Schueller was both ideologue and financier. In 1948, Corrèze was sentenced to twenty years in prison.

As for Jacques Corrèze, 'he didn't knock at the door of L'Oréal by accident. He sought out the help of his old friend and supporter Eugène Schueller, with whom he shared the leadership of La Cagoule and the MSR. Schueller, the financer of both fascist movements, the founder of

L'Oréal, was already by the early 1950s one of the richest men in France.'[61]

In his book, Michel Bar-Zohar mentions Jacques Corrèze's *cagoulard* past and his prison sentence for murder. He also delineates the quite strange way in which Corrèze bought the Helena Rubinstein Company on behalf of L'Oréal. He explains how Corrèze and other ex-Nazis found refuge as employees in different branches of L'Oréal. Corrèze's trajectory after the war is exemplary in that respect. He was first of all vice-chairman of Procasa, the Spanish branch of L'Oréal. Then he cropped up again in South America where he worked for a local branch of the group. It was then that he found his way to New York. Soon after he had arrived, he was appointed chair of the new company Cosmair, the exclusive representative of L'Oréal in the United States.

It was there moreover that he got to know Helena Rubinstein from whom he carefully concealed his past. He saw her a lot and managed to become a friend. Executioners will do anything to attract their prey: apparently Eichmann spoke fluent Yiddish and used this language to confuse the Jews he subsequently exterminated.

Upon Helena Rubinstein's death, Corrèze plotted cunningly and, by using pseudonyms and front companies, he discreetly bought the latter's eponymous company, all on behalf of L'Oréal. When the deal was completed, he became chairman of the Helena Rubinstein Company.[62]

During this time L'Oréal was expanding its capital in Karlsruhe. I have to hand the *Stuttgarter Zeitung* for June 14 1979 that the archive service at the town hall sent me. According to this newspaper's calculations, L'Oréal's capital by the end of 1978 totalled 4.3 billion DM. And we were still only in 1978…

---

61 Michel Bar-Zohar, *Une histoire sans fard: L'Oréal des années sombres au boycott arabe*, pp. 56-61.'
62 Ibid., p. 110.

19

An Epidemic of Amnesia

I didn't always understand why our adversaries strove to deny everything. I could accept they might try to pull the wool over our eyes; they were big companies and could allow themselves that luxury. Such an attitude has its limits, and when one is caught, as they say, with one's hand in the till, one should try to find a honourable solution rather than continue denying the evidence.

Our powerful interlocutors should have known that people of modest means wouldn't take lightly the risk of writing to them and that if they did take the risk it was because they had solid evidence to back their case.

In this respect, I would like to return to one of their lies: the famous signature that my great-uncle, Karl Rosenfelder, was supposed to have placed on the 1951 agreement. He never signed it! But even if they had secured it, nobody could ever accept that, in order to buy a house with two owners (Karl and my mother), a single signature would suffice. One doesn't need to have studied law to know that property belonging to two people and sold by only one of them constitutes a sale that is null and void. The 1951 agreement reached between BGV and a Jewish organization endorsing the sale of the house for 5,000 DM also contained an article number 3 that rendered it null if the legal owners appeared.

The truth is that they have no valid arguments on their side and that the only weapon they can wield is intimidation. Their arguments are fallacious; here are some more that are much more convincing – mine:

The extracts from the property register show that this house belonged to us in 1938.

The transfer documents from the Nazi era prove the transfer was obtained under constraint (that is even written into the bill of *purchase*). It was because his life and the life of his relatives were threatened that my grandfather yielded to blackmail.

The money arising from this enforced sale was never paid either to my grandparents or their heirs.

In the normal course of things, this stolen property should then have been returned after the war. They must have forgotten about us!

One bank also had an attack of amnesia around the same time. The document originating from the police in Lyons[63] contained interesting information, as well as a physical description of my grandfather: Fritz was carrying a supply of cash on him and could get money outside the camp. This had enabled him to get permission (one can guess how) to leave the Gurs camp for a few days in order to visit a cousin in Lyons. The police inspector who drew up the report states he had a sum in dollars deposited in an account with the Société générale in Paris.

I contacted the Société générale to find out about this account; they replied that the bank had no knowledge of my grandfather. How then could I explain that an official document – I didn't invent it, it exists in the Alpes-Maritimes provincial archives – mentioned that this account existed?

What I found really disturbing was that yet again any trace of my grandparents was being denied. This process has been repeated too often for me not to ask serious questions about the divulging of information by official bodies. Similarly, whenever the Drai Commission[64] pointed me to ministries in order to find information, the doors to these institutions

---

63 See Chapter 10.

64 This is the commission set up to compensate victims of thefts perpetrated under the anti-Semitic legislation passed during the Occupation. The commission was a result of the Matteoli Report. When the person responsible for my dossier contacted me, on behalf of the prime minister, this commission hadn't yet been officially established.

mysteriously closed as soon as they heard my requests: they could find nothing, not a scrap of documentation mentioning that my grandparents existed. If I were to believe them, the latter never lived in France or evaporated discreetly together with the documents that related to them. Could the fact that André Bettencourt was at the head of several of these ministries be connected to this situation?

It just so happens that one of Bettencourt's friends, a director in his time of the Société générale, was implicated in the Frydman affair.

Luckily for us, there are always breakdowns in the almost reflex practice of withholding information: everything isn't entirely fixed and, by making an effort, you always finds in the end someone helpful – in this or that archive service – who will give you more or less officially the information the official organizations have refused you at least up to now…

The person in charge of research into banks for the Drai Commission, to whom I had sent the document from the Lyons police, called me soon after. The activity of the commission in relation to the Société générale had borne fruit: the bank had just discovered a foreign-currency account in the name of Fritz Rosenfelder but was unable to say what amount was held there.

I have just received the written response that the Société générale supplied the commission. If I possess the proof that I haven't invented anything, I continue to be quite puzzled by the bank's attitude. They recognize the existence of a foreign-currency account in my grandparents' name but don't consider they need to return the sum credited on the pretext that 'it was reactivated after the war'. Well, at that time my entire family was dead, and my mother, a minor, had left for Brazil without ever setting foot back in France. I can see no other explanation for reactivating this account other than the fact that these gentlemen believe in ghosts!

L'Oréal's ability to hide the truth never ceases to astonish me. *Maître* Zaoui was also astonished: not as far as our case was concerned but during the Touvier trial, scenes from which were broadcast on the History Channel. He fulminated, in the course of his defence of the civil parties, at the Nazis' impressive ability to hide the truth: that is, to lie. He even gave a name to this skill: '*ignorance*'. He recalled how during the Frankfurt trial,

Mr Hoffman[65], the head of Auschwitz, denied any knowledge of what was happening in his camp and pretended that they were only making sandbags for children...

---

[65] This trial was held from 1963 to 1965. The camp commandants and their deputies were tried. *Maître Zaoui* quotes an extract from sworn statements from the trial.

20

Nightmares

The repeated denials I had to confront took their toll on my sleep; I became prey to nightmares.

The scenes were horrific. I saw things, although I'd never lived them. I see myself running from the Nazis, I see aeroplanes in flames and incinerated bodies, I see myself behind barbed wire among people who survive, although they have been deprived of their right to live, I see details of uniforms, fragments of emaciated faces, I see... I feel a sharp pain... I smell smells... I'm suddenly transported to an era that I never knew and yet it all seems real.

I have the impression that when my mother was carrying me in her belly she passed her fears on to me and that my body has retained a memory of them. This memory is all the more intense because it passes through a body exercised by years of energetic dancing.

I've slept very little for five years, as if to spare myself these nightmares. Which nevertheless don't appear by chance: they also tell stories, and I discover things I never knew.

I went to see Roman Polanski's *The Pianist* when it was released, a film bearing witness to the life of the Polish pianist Wladyslaw Szpilman in the Warsaw ghetto. I thought it was a wonderful film. From a strictly cinematic point of view, the director is undoubtedly a great filmmaker who has married technical expertise and artistic sensibility: it is a masterpiece! I felt that I was in step with the story, and seeing it did me a power of good: I had the feeling that Polanski had lived the situation from within, that someone could understand what I was experiencing. My reaction was all the stronger because I remembered my very first job at the Paris Opéra. I had been one of Polanski's assistants when he'd produced *The Tales of Hoffmann*, the opera by Jacques Offenbach. I didn't know, at the time, that he was Jewish or had a past related to the Shoah. And vice versa.

I am very happy that he was awarded the *Palme d'Or* in Cannes. It was well deserved.

I have always loved going to the cinema. The art of film enthralls and entertains me. Moreover, indirectly it helps me in my work. But ever since I started this research, I go to the cinema less and less. I find some films insipid while others suddenly really scare me, yet years ago they would have had made much less impression: I would have reassured myself by saying it's only 'a film'. Nonetheless, I think that no scriptwriter is capable of imagining the perfidious machinations certain people are able to perpetrate in real life.

All this was making me so ill that my mother at one stage asked me to give it all up.

I've already mentioned the fears expressed by friends and relatives on the dangers I was exposing myself to by setting out on such an enterprise. I was attacking something much more powerful than myself, I was entering a zone where money and collusion are bedfellows and risked losing feathers in the process. Both in France and Brazil, several friends tried to dissuade me from running such a risk.

In the light of certain facts I have gradually discovered and incidents that I have experienced personally, I have come to understand that certain things don't just happen in the cinema. I was very naïve to think France was beyond this kind of thing. Years of dictatorship in Brazil had led me to expect something different from a democracy. But too often money sweeps away beliefs it finds in its path and, as soon as it imposes its rule, it puts in place a much subtler regime than any dictatorship: the sight of money makes people bow and shut their eyes. And don't the French say that the worst blind man is the one who refuses to see? The other day, in the supermarket near my house, more than six policemen went to arrest a mildly retarded man who had stolen something to eat. The woman at the till was so shocked she offered, unsuccessfully, to pay out of her own pocket so they didn't take him off. When it comes to the poor, the law *is* applied...

Despite the anxiety that sometimes overwhelms me whenever someone asks or advises me to throw in the towel, I always tell myself: 'No! I won't give up. We are in the right. We must fight on behalf of this right. Otherwise, my family will have died for nothing. Otherwise, those who struggled to defend an ideal, the fighters in the Resistance (the real ones), the people who saved my mother, all these people will have fought for nothing. I owe it to them to show a minimum of courage.'

But I'm not the only one who needs courage, and I wonder daily whether the justice system will also be courageous. Will it dare to put a powerful multinational on trial – even if I have all the evidence to prove its alleged guilt – with all the likely political consequences that will bring?

To round everything off, L'Oréal informed us that our action would be inadmissible because the incriminating facts are invalidated by prescription. If such were the case, the prescription would serve as a pretext and not as the real reason for their inadmissibility.

The notion of prescription can be interpreted in different ways. My grandparents died in the Holocaust, which is considered to be a crime against humanity, and hence one that can never be prescribed by the passage of time. We presented an action against the receiving and retention of stolen property. As L'Oréal has kept the profits from this receiving of stolen goods[66], namely the profits from the sale of a house stolen by the Nazis, there is no prescription. But, as I have just said, there can be different interpretations. And if the legal system reckons the case is too delicate, it will find a way of seeing it off. It can judge things from the opposite perspective: an entrance can also be an exit. But you need to have the will to go in, and there lies the rub: does the system want justice to be done? Is the law the same for both the weak and the strong?

---

66 Under French law, the receiving and keeping of stolen goods is what is called a 'continuous crime' that only ceases when the property is restored. It is only from this moment that the calculation of the three-year limit begins.

I lived under a military dictatorship for most of that part of my life I lived in Brazil. I had time to understand how dictators have recourse to violence because they have no other way of doing things.

There were certainly some ridiculous sides to the Brazilian system of repression. Everything Russian was forbidden on principle: 'Russian' meant 'Communism' and thus subversion. It was on this basis that works written before the Communist period were often banned until the censors realized they were making fools of themselves and authorized the publication of books like Dostoyevsky's *Crime and Punishment* or Tolstoy's *Anna Karenina*. But the preposterous side to censorship wasn't enough to make ordinary citizens forget the constraints imposed by the dictatorship and, in particular, the fact that it was extremely difficult to leave the country. The restriction was subtler than a simple ban on leaving the country as practised by Eastern Bloc countries; whoever wanted to leave the country had to pay out a fortune and leave a cash deposit; consequently, only well-off Brazilians could afford such a luxury.

There is something else I had grasped about dictators. They are people who are perfectly integrated into society. They are 'good fathers', married to 'charming wives' and have 'devoted staff'. Of course, people under their orders torture and rape, particularly intellectuals, but at the same time, their wives do charity work and hence put into their charitable endeavours a minute part of the money they have stolen from the people in order to bolster their Swiss bank accounts. Thus, despite the torture and pillage, they are thought to be remarkable individuals and are invited to the best dinner parties.

21

Masquerade

Mr Owen-Jones sent my mother a letter on 4 October 2001[67]. Whenever I reread it, it disgusts me. Firstly because of its oh-so-sophisticated trappings. Secondly because of its content.

When the letter arrived, I was astonished to receive a letter from Owen-Jones sent to my house since his lawyers had been in contact with ours who had contacted him. It was as if L'Oréal's chief executive thought we didn't need a lawyer!

Before I opened the envelope I drew my first naïve conclusion: they've understood! They've understood that we hold irrefutable proof and that they cannot escape their responsibilities. Owen-Jones is writing to me at home to ask us to forgive him. He must be wanting to suggest a peaceful solution in order to calm the waters.

When I started to read the letter, I didn't immediately change my state of mind; I found his tone pleasant, even friendly, and human. But I very soon realized that that was the point of his manoeuvre. In effect, his honeyed tone was only a ploy, to put my mother and me at ease.

Unfortunately for Mr Owen-Jones, I knew my dossier by heart and very quickly spotted the tissue of lies hiding behind by his friendly tone. This gentleman has a gift for making a travesty of truth, for making documents say the opposite of what they mean. Despite, the letter's most

67 See Appendix 11.

urbane veneer, I felt it was insulting. Far from sending us a private letter to offer his apologies, he had written to convince my mother that neither in the past nor today was L'Oréal at all responsible for the theft of our house. I was scandalized and called my lawyer:

'*Maître*, how can you let them send me a cheap letter like this?'

I felt that my fury had fazed him, even though, I think, he understood the reasons driving it.

'Madame, I understand you are angry, but is that a reason for you to lose your temper with your lawyer who, may I remind you, is on your side?'

I knew in my heart of hearts that he was right, but I wanted to hear him express his disgust. I calmed down and we were able to discuss the content of the letter and the attitude we should adopt. I asked him to wait before we reached a decision, because as always when I am in a rage, I need time to stand back and think level-headedly.

As I was rereading the letter, the documents that proved Mr Owen-Jones's bad faith paraded round my head.

I quote: 'In 1954, the L'Oréal subsidiary in Germany, in which the group bought back shares only in 1961…'

To mention 1961 is a way of locating the event at a far remove from the war and the Vichy government: as if to say, L'Oréal had no connections whatsoever with the Nazis. As if I didn't know the truth! And didn't Mme Bettencourt hold 95 percent of the shares in Haarfarben? And wasn't François Dalle, the chief executive of L'Oréal in France, also the managing director of L'Oréal in Germany? And what about André Tondu, the founder of Haarfarben und Parfümerien?

The letter sent to me and not to my lawyer was therefore an official response. And I can demonstrate its lies. Mr Owen-Jones didn't, of course, suspect that I had got the documents from the company registry. With great difficulty, it is true, and by sheer persistence, but I did succeed in the end. These documents prove, as I have already said, that in 1959, 95 percent of the capital in Haarfarben und Parfümerien was owned by Mrs Bettencourt, née Liliane Schueller.

Subsequently, I found a document from the French administration confirming that Haarfarben belonged to L'Oréal well before 1959. Today

I can hold this document in my hands and state categorically that Owen-Jones, by trying to hide the fact that Haarfarben already belonged to L'Oréal in 1954 – the date when our house was purchased – and by lying so outrageously in the letter sent to my home in October 2001, is trying to protect the subsidiary from any fallout. It is what is known as 'complicity in the possession of stolen goods'.

And must we remind Mr Owen-Jones that the L'Oréal in Germany website – a fact legally recognized by a public lawyer – relates how André Tondu was ordered by Eugène Schueller in 1930 to found Haarfarben, first in Berlin and then in Karlsruhe in 1945. Schueller gave out orders from Paris. André Tondu carried them out in Germany. Haarfarben was secretly L'Oréal in Germany. And we will soon discover how André Tondu was officially employed by L'Oréal from at least 1948.

When in 1954 André Tondu bought back from BGV, on behalf of Haarfarben und Parfümerien, the house that had been stolen from us by the Nazis, he was then fully representing L'Oréal. And if the purchase only became effective from 1954, it was because it couldn't be enacted before then. In fact, as we have seen, and as I will repeat to refresh our memories, L'Oréal had coveted the house at Wendstrasse 19 at least from 1948. Under the orders of Eugène Schueller, Ensa – the front company for L'Oréal, managed by André Tondu – signed two different bills of purchase for number 17, the neighbouring house, although it only paid once. The first bill dates from February 1949, the second is signed 5 November 1951, the same day as the pseudo-agreement was signed between BGV and a Jewish association in relation to our house[68]. And, on exactly the same day, Haarfarben-L'Oréal was buying the other house contiguous to ours, number 18 Kaiserallee. To conclude the transaction that would enable L'Oréal to build its German headquarters on the three adjacent lots, the company had merely to buy our house. This series of transactions only made sense if they purchased the middle property: ours. It seems clear then, since the neighbouring properties had been bought outright, that L'Oréal was sure it was going to get

---

68 See Appendices 7 and 8.

Wendstrasse 19: something that the laws on stolen property had made impossible till then.

I will continue my analysis of the letter from Owen-Jones. I quote: 'In 1951, a Jewish association, legally appointed to take the place of the Jews exterminated by the Nazi regime...' Except that, in the event, we are dealing here not with a Jewish woman who has been exterminated but one who couldn't be more alive. The proof: he's writing to her. If in 2001 L'Oréal is still able to deny her existence, you can understand the difficulty my mother has always experienced in accepting she has a right to be alive.

To continue: '...and your uncle [...] signed an agreement with the insurance company...' But where is my great-uncle Karl's signature? Above all, where is my mother's signature? Nowhere to be found![69] And, as he mentions my great-uncle, he thus acknowledges his existence, and he himself makes this clear: L'Oréal knew he was alive in 1951. What Owen-Jones doesn't say – and what I've learned afterwards, thanks to other documents – is that my great-uncle not only didn't sign the agreement but also died several years later in dire poverty.

Another document exists to which I have yet to refer: an internal BGV document mentioning the Nazi lawyer[70] who was supposedly speaking on behalf of my great-uncle. This lawyer, Dr Sickinger, had already crossed with my family: as chairman of the group of national-socialist lawyers of the Karlsruhe district in the Nazi era[71], he was the main person responsible for banning my grandfather, Fritz – himself a lawyer – from practising. Sickinger is, by this token, the third player in this case directly linked to the Third Reich. His presence is then no chance thing; he was a very efficient ally when it came to keeping Karl away from the agreement allowing them to rob him and us. The internal BGV memo reveals this sleight-of-hand. It shows that Sickinger openly sided with BGV: 'If an

---

69 See Appendix 8.

70 I have in my possession several letters sent by Dr Sickinger that end with 'Heil Hitler!'

71 See Appendix 13.

agreement proves impossible, *Maître* Sickinger will renounce his brief for he has no wish to intervene against us [BGV].[72]' BGV was in possession of this document, and so was L'Oréal.

Everything was arranged in advance, so that the only outcome possible would be to turn the three plots of land into one. And this manoeuvre was carried out long after the Nazi period as if the events of history had no impact on the power of those responsible: a post-war manoeuvre that also represented a whitewash of BGV's Nazi past.

I had lulled myself with false expectations that the present generation would regret the actions of its parents. Nothing had changed.

Counter-truth followed on half-truths, and it would be too lengthy and repetitious to mention every detail. But I will quote the end of the letter. It gave me a cruel insight into the lack of respect towards my mother and made me realize that hypocrisy knows no bounds:

'I would not want you to imagine that my attitude is dictated by a wish to delay matters, that is why I am very happy to contribute towards the expenses you might accrue in your researches in Germany and consultations necessary for the preparation of your dossier.

If you accept this offer, the aim of which is to help you in your search for the truth…'

And he concludes by inviting us to make contact with him or his lawyers.

When I read this passage, I leaped out of my chair: Mr Owen-Jones had crossed the line! Search for the truth? Documents? We already had everything. And these documents clearly indict L'Oréal. The truth is there!

What I find really indecent in his proposal is that L'Oréal deprived my mother of the enjoyment of her property and still dares to deny her: an old lady who lived the Shoah in her flesh and in her soul! Owen-Jones continues:

'A theft constitutes an intolerable attack on the rights of human beings and must certainly be redressed. I am personally committed to the group I head being above reproach.'

---

72 See Appendix 12.

My friends jokingly began to advise me to take care. I think some were really worried. They asked me if I had given photocopies of the documents I'd collected to different trustworthy people. That made me laugh, and I retorted that they'd seen too many police films, even though I had in fact copied the documents and lodged them in a safe place. I was also told that I was naïve: that these people were capable of doing things you imagine impossible in a state of law.

Mr Erwin Brunner, the director of BGV who – under the Nazi regime – had taken over our house, had managed to get a whitewash from a denazification trial. Mr Owen-Jones – the chief executive of L'Oréal, which bought our house from BGV as if it belonged to this company – was content to write a letter and relieve his company of all responsibility, even though we had supplied him with all the documents proving that this house belonged to us, as well as evidence showing that L'Oréal had acquired a property stolen by the Nazis...

At the time I received this letter, which I was to forward to my mother, the refurbishing of a production of *Rigoletto* at the Opéra-Bastille was proving to be very time-consuming. The September 11 attacks had taken place the month before, and the psychosis gripping American airports led to the cancellation of several flights. Hence, some singers couldn't arrive on the dates agreed, and rehearsals had to begin late. I wasn't particularly distressed by this hitch in the preparations for the opera – it is something that happens frequently in my trade, and I know how to handle it – although I'd have to pull out all the stops to conclude the rehearsals on time. From now on it was the responsibility of the courts to deliver a verdict on L'Oréal's lies. No doubt I shouldn't have waited so long to take action, but now my conscience was peaceful. I had offered our adversaries every possible opportunity to reach an honourable settlement; they showed not the slightest interest. At no time did I play the game of 'an eye for an eye, a tooth for a tooth'. I always went out of my way to show respect towards them, but they showed us none. I'd given them a chance, but they had only laughed at us.

'*Maître*, enough is enough. You're right: we must take them to court!'

22

My Grandfather

My mother sent me a manuscript that my grandfather, Fritz, wrote when he was lodged in a Swiss prison after he had escaped from France. He had scrawled it on bits of paper that came his way. The style is stiff, if not laborious, and that makes the document occasionally difficult to understand. He couldn't know that after the war people would talk about the Holocaust, but you can sense his desire to bear witness, to leave evidence so people would know.

His account is extremely reserved, and certain facts are never explicitly mentioned. But the man who is writing is also afraid: he takes care never to give the real names of the people to whom he refers – to the point of travestying his own identity. Moreover, you can discern a good number of anachronisms. Was it his state of health (his stays in the camps made him incurably ill) that led him to speak of my grandmother in 1943, when she was deported and died in 1942? Or was it a deliberate intention on his part to alter the dates of certain events?

Nevertheless, what strikes me most about this manuscript is the daily struggle he engaged in, like others, to preserve his dignity as a human being. He recounts a squabble among prisoners over a potato floating in a watery soup in one of the camps he passed through. He refused to join in the squabble over a morsel of potato with people who shared his fate, even though he was as hungry as they were and had already lost fifteen kilos (he was to lose even more).

He describes moments when he is caught between his own need to survive and the help he feels he must give to those who are in a worse state and recalls that, at such moments, to think only of oneself is to abdicate from one's condition as a civilized human being and thus admit the Nazis and collaborators are right.

He speaks of his anguish in the camp at Gurs when he discovers an aunt of his, who had fallen victim to the dysentery that was rife at the time, in one of the small blocks of cabins where the prisoners were lodged. More than ten people were dying from it everyday. He bribed a guard in order to get into the female section. The critical state of his aunt and other women made him desperate.

The temperature was several degrees below zero, and he managed to gather a few men together to stop the gaps in the walls with mud as best they could so that it wasn't so cold in the cabin. One man had matches that allowed them to make a fire and warm some stones they then placed on the women's bellies like hot water bottles, thus saving several lives. His aunt, however, did not survive.

Other members of the family arrived in the camp. My grandfather recounts how he bartered in order to get a blanket for an uncle who was shivering with cold. But by the time he finally got the blanket, his uncle was already dead.

His narrative relates other similar incidents with members of the family. People were dropping like flies.

He also speaks of the decision he reached with friends to organize evenings of lectures, variety shows and concerts (there were well known artistes in the camp), so their fellow detainees didn't forget they were human beings and life didn't resign them to their condition as prisoners. These nocturnal activities enabled them to cling to life and find the strength to struggle on.

My grandfather was imprisoned several times in the camp at Les Milles, near Aix-en-Provence. Apart from his manuscript, several documents attest to this series of internments.

During his last stay there, he learned he was on a list to be deported to Auschwitz and decided to escape. He had money on him, as he had taken care not to give everything to the camp chief on his arrival. This money enabled him to get things from time to time. It allowed him to help those who had less than him, usually nothing at all.

One of his friends and fellow detainees gave him a tip-off: one guard, in exchange for money, had agreed to shut his eyes, but only at night. And that was how my grandfather's escape was organized.

The camp at Les Milles was an old brick factory and had a big chimney that was out of action. The top of the conduit had been blocked to prevent escape attempts, but the two men had spotted a recess inside, which could act as a hiding-place for my grandfather. It would be a very perilous undertaking: apart from the inevitable risk of being caught or falling, he would have to spend several days in an uncomfortable position and disregard his natural needs. But Fritz had nothing to lose and hid there while waiting for the night when the bribed guard would be on duty.

He had some anxious moments in his hiding-place, notably when the police came to inspect the chimney. He was a hairsbreadth away from being discovered, the dogs had sniffed him, and the police swept the conduit with their torches, but luckily for him, without success.

It was after this episode that his friend informed him he could come out of hiding (they'd agreed to sound a signal). Fritz and his companions had made a kind of theatre stage with scenery made from materials they'd recycled from the camp. This stage had a trapdoor that opened down to a cellar, at the end of which was the door controlled by the guard. Fritz gave him money in exchange for opening the door and thus found himself free once again, at least for a while.

In relation to this guard, my grandfather writes in his manuscript: 'He tries to efface by night the suffering he causes by day.'

My grandfather then went to Allauch, where his wife Kaethe and daughter Edith were living. When he got there, he learned the French gendarmes had just rounded up his wife and that she had been incarcerated in the camp at Les Milles. His daughter had managed to escape; she had been lucky not to be in Allauch that day; and Rosette, a young girl from the village, went to save her in Marseille, where she'd gone with her school teacher. While keeping out of sight of the French police, my grandfather went to recover his daughter. He also tried to organize his wife's escape, but to no avail.

My mother has visited me once since I've been living in France. It was in July 1988. We hired a car and went to the south east of France for a week. She wanted me to get to know this region. At the time, I knew nothing about her past, and when I saw her in an emotional state, I just put it down to her reaction to the little discoveries we kept making. I was far from imagining that it was finding herself back in this region with her own daughter that provoked the emotion. We didn't go to Allauch…

We'd agreed that, because of my work, at the end of our stay I'd go back to Paris by train and she'd go to Marseille by herself and return the car. When the time came to say goodbye, she suddenly became nervous and said in a childish voice: 'I can never drive the car by myself to Marseille.'

I couldn't understand the reasons for her distress because she had done the driving from the start of our holiday. And she knew that my international driving licence was no longer valid and that I couldn't take the wheel.

'Mum, you know I can't drive legally. What will I say if there's a police check?'

And she replied quite seriously: 'You just tell them you're with your mother and that everything is fine.'

I burst out laughing (she didn't understand why), but there was no way I could drive. We went our separate ways and, to soothe her anxieties, I promised to be near a telephone as soon as I returned to Paris, so she could catch up with me.

I'd totally misunderstood what she was going through. I even told her shortly after how I'd been completely at a loss. But at no time did she tell me she'd lived near Marseille, nor what it meant for her to go back there by herself after so many years.

I felt very guilty when I recently discovered this page from her childhood and understood why she was so anxious that day. I hope she'll be able to return to France; next time, we'll go to Marseille and come back together.

23

Media Reaction

The indictment was ready. Now my mother had only to read and sign it. I sent it to her by FedEx, but she sent it back by Sedex, a kind of Brazilian DHL. Three weeks went by, and it still hadn't arrived. It was December, the end-of-year festivities were nigh, and Sedex in Brazil had more business than it could cope with. I sent the indictment back to Brazil, and my mother finally despatched it to us by FedEx. In this way, the indictment was finally lodged on 28 December 2001.

There are moments when *maître* Korman is less available because of the other cases he has to see to. So I had to champ the bit while waiting for him to be free again. I was, moreover, intensely annoyed by the bureaucratic hold-ups that delayed the despatch of documents I had ordered. To placate my impatience, I went to the Bibliothèque nationale and asked for everything they had related to L'Oréal. But whenever one wants to consult this kind of documentation, there are special formalities to be completed at the Bibliothèque nationale. They can't be sorted in a minute, and by the time I got my pass, the library was closing its doors. I came back as soon I had some free time, and on this occasion when it was open.

The first documents that I read ranged from different ways to use hair dyes to old hairdressing magazines. Then I came across the magazine of the L'Oréal joint production committee for November 1948. This magazine, entitled *Au Cap*, carried a page on 'Our Company' which spoke of the company's different branches throughout the world including 'Haarfarben, first based in Berlin, now in Karlsruhe, with Mr Tondu as its manager as always'. It ended with the motto: 'L'Oréal everywhere, L'Oréal forever, L'Oréal always…' Indeed!

Until then all I had on André Tondu was the document I'd found on the L'Oréal website. They were still pretending Mr Tondu was not involved with L'Oréal, that he was not a company employee! The production committee magazine gives quite a different picture; and in a pile of documents I found another issue of the same magazine: this time for March 1949. There were stories on the 1948 Christmas parties, and notably the end-of-year party at Haarfarben und Parfümerien which took place on 11 December in Karlsruhe: 'We give thanks to the kind Mr Tondu, our friend as always, for sending the texts written by staff on the occasion of this event.'[73] This gentleman really had a very strange close relationship with the mother company for someone reduced to the rank of lowly estate agent by Mr Owen-Jones and his lawyers! It was quite clear in my view that he was working actively for the group, beyond the mere duties of middleman that they attempted to confer on him, and that he must really be well acquainted with the production committee (and vice versa) for the latter to dub him a friend.

Now the press had to be informed. I had no contacts in this milieu, and when I phoned the newspapers directly I got no joy. I quickly understood that you had to mention the name of a journalist in order to cross the threshold of an editorial board. Once again I turned to my friends for help. Two gave me the names of journalists to contact on their behalf. But even with this strong insider support, my case was far from getting a hearing.

I first met with the director of a television news team, and he welcomed me most warmly. He suggested the topic to one of his reporters. The latter meticulously reviewed my fifty-centimetre-high pile of documents. It took him almost a month to complete the task. It is true that our respective timetables didn't always allow us to meet up quickly when he needed me to explain some of the detail. I felt I was already in

---

73 See Appendices 15 and 16.

court because – if he believed my story after he'd read everything – like everyone else, he started out by doubting it was true. It was the beginning of February 2002. The reporter then told me that he wanted to take on the story and we'd both have to go to Karlsruhe. But before that, he had two other reports to finish. From the beginning of March, I was the one not available: I had to go and stay in Toulouse for fifty days in order to create a big opera. Nevertheless, he was the first journalist to take an interest in my case and want to work on it.

His editorial boss warned me of the difficulty of the project. L'Oréal is the premier advertiser in France, and the vast majority of the daily, weekly or television press needs this advertising manna. He warmed my heart when he assured me that, in spite of this, he would fight to get the subject on air.

In the meantime, after I'd sent a synopsis of the case to journalists, I got two appointments. The first meeting went extremely well, and the journalist promised his article would be out the following week. The second, also a journalist working for a big daily, gave me an appointment for the Thursday after our telephone conversation on a Monday. Two hours after we'd spoken, he rang back. He'd just spoken to L'Oréal by phone as his duty as a journalist required. He'd mentioned some of the synopsis, which had led to his call. L'Oréal had asked him to send them a copy. He was calling back to see if I had any objections. Additionally, even though L'Oréal did admit they were acquainted with the story, their spokesman had told him he knew nothing of any action being been brought against the group. At that moment, I leaped in: 'What are they talking about? There they go again, saying they don't know a thing! Of course an action has been started against them. My lawyer had sent a letter to L'Oréal's two lawyers alerting them to the indictment, and I myself wrote to Mr Owen-Jones to inform him that the only response his letter to my mother deserved was court action. And yet they say they have only "heard" about this story! I'm astonished at their ability to adapt reality. I can show you all this correspondence.'

The journalist was intrigued by my reactions.

'Can we meet up this afternoon rather than Thursday?'

'Of course.'

We arranged to meet in a café a few hours later. I showed him the very first letter from my lawyer dated June 2001, the one from the L'Oréal's Chief Executive and then mine telling Mr Owen-Jones we would meet in court. I started to relate my story by showing one by one the documents I had brought with me. I was beginning to anticipate this kind of exercise and had prepared a book of photos. He asked questions and wanted further explanations of certain points he found difficult to fathom.

We then went to his newspaper office to make photocopies. But I hadn't brought all my documentation. I'd already told him how extensive that was, and even if I had brought everything, he wouldn't have been able to read them all in a few hours. He also wanted to check everything. We agreed to meet again and that I'd bring him more documents. He scrutinized them all before making fresh contact with L'Oréal and their lawyers; he had questions he wanted to put to them. He also questioned my lawyer. We saw each other once more because he wanted to check some final points before the article appeared.

In the meantime, I'd called back the first journalist, who'd promised there would be an article in his newspaper the following week. But his tone of voice told me he'd had a change of mind. I work with voices, and it is rare for me to miss this kind of thing. In the eyes of my interlocutor, 'things weren't that clear', 'we weren't sure'. He didn't ask for any extra documents, and I realized I couldn't count on him to write an article for his newspaper.

After presenting his article to his superiors, the second journalist kept me up to date on its probable appearance. Every two days it was the same scenario: 'It won't be out tomorrow, perhaps the day after.' Even if he said nothing, I felt he was fighting. There were days when his voice betrayed dejection, others when I felt he was hopeful, but at no time did his tone change in relation to me. He repeated his reports on possible publication for three weeks until one day – I'd only been in Toulouse for a few days, when he called me: 'It's coming out tomorrow. We've succeeded!'

I was extremely happy. The curtain of secrecy was going to be lifted, and people would finally know what had happened.

The article, entitled 'The Daughter of Deported Parents Accuses L'Oréal of Profiting from Land in Karlsruhe Stolen from Her Family in 1938', appeared in *Le Monde* on 8 March, 2002. It was accompanied by a photo of our house in Karlsruhe. There was a second article, entitled 'Edith Rosenfelder's Long Quest to Find the House of her Childhood'. A small article referred to the Frydman affair.

I must pay particular homage to this newspaper and its journalist, Alexandre García, because it required lots of courage to publish this article. Respecting honour and ethics is a daily battle. 'It has taken men thousands of years to stand up. What would life be worth if it were conducted at ground level?' These sentences[74] would have been a perfect compliment, if they hadn't been uttered by Mrs Bettencourt, who simply forgot to match words with deeds.

I got calls from all over. Brazilian newspapers even contacted me. Those I spoke to have followed up the subject. But not a single press organ in France reacted.

L'Oréal viewed the appearance of the article as a form of blackmail. To be sure, I have numerous faults, I'm impulsive, I don't have an easy character, I can even sometimes be intolerable – as my detractors say – but I am thoroughly honest and would never dream of practising blackmail in order to get money.

I was married to a very rich man, and if money were my motive, I would have accepted the settlement his father offered me when we separated. But I refused it: I thought I had no right to such a thing.

You say, this is blackmail? No! We are simply asking you to give back what belongs to us, and we say that what you call blackmail is only justice.

---

[74] Reported by Bruno Abescat, *La Saga des Bettencourt*, op. cit.

24

My Grandmother

I did get to know Marianne, my great-aunt. Just before she died she whispered a few words to me about her sister-in-law, Kaethe, whom she had met. She spoke to me of a beautiful, very elegant women. She also told me what she felt about my grandmother's deportation. According to her, Kaethe couldn't stand more escape attempts and humiliations and simply resigned herself to her fate.

When I was given Kaethe's deportation book at the Centre for Contemporary Jewish Documentation, people encouraged me to go to the National Archives in Paris; I might come across important information there. So I went and was well received and advised on how to pursue my researches: I was given some microfilm by the man responsible for that section, who then added that the photocopier was free for victims of the Shoah and their heirs. I appreciated that gesture as a form of recognition.

I kept dropping the microfilm and couldn't manage the simple operation of slotting it into the machine. I was embarrassed, and my hands were shaking. The section head smiled and came to my rescue.

'I'm sorry, I'm really clumsy and can't keep still,' I told him. He slipped the film into the machine, showed me how it worked, then asked me what my grandmother's surname was before leaving me to my researches.

I began to process an alphabetical list of names of individuals with their age, family status and place of residence. Endless columns of men, women and children of all ages began to pass before me. Sometimes it was a whole family. These people came from all over: from France but also from the rest of Europe. What they had in common was that they'd all transited through the camp in Drancy before being sent usually to Auschwitz. I mentally pictured them saying goodbye to each other, clutching their suitcases full of personal effects which would later be confiscated. These effects were mentioned on the microfilm.

My head was in a whirl. I couldn't manage to get the machine to stay on 'Rosenfelder'. The section head came to my rescue once again, but I found I was unable to continue reading immediately. I had to get up and walk round. When I returned, I did succeed in reading: 'Kaethe Rosenfelder née Hirsch, 6 rue des Saussaies, convoy number 29.'

Although the document made no mention of personal effects, I did, however, register the epithet 'head of family'. The French police at the time was well informed: this detail was quite in order since she had become the head of family after the repeated absences of my grandfather, who was moving from one camp to another.

We looked for other microfilms related to my search, but to no avail. Anyway, my emotions on this occasion overrode my wish to continue; I had found my reference, and after thanking my saviour and making a few photocopies, I left the building so I could breathe normally once more.

I sent my brother a copy of our grandmother Kaethe's deportation book. I wanted him to share my emotions. I had taken the precaution beforehand of making him promise he wouldn't under any circumstance show this document to my mother.

Two or three days went by before he rang me on Sunday afternoon.

'Hallo, how's it going?'

'Fine…'

He started to reel off his news: he was going to work in the south of Brazil, etc. He spoke non-stop, but I felt he was going round in circles. Once he'd exhausted all the subjects that came to mind, I could only add a banal: 'Fine, we'll be in touch. Love.'

He sensed I was about to hang up.

'By the way, the documents concerning Grandmother…'

He's taken his time, I told myself. That was typical of him: he was incapable of saying they had bowled him over, and he needed to speak about the first thing that came into his head to hide his real feelings. Nonetheless, we spoke about them and finally he exclaimed: 'They must give us our house back! What do they think they're playing at? Can you take somebody's house just because you want it?'

I laughed at his way of putting it, but, essentially, it was exactly that: what did they think they were playing at by simply appropriating a house that belonged to somebody else?

In July 2002, I went to Aix-en-Provence for the annual song festival. The camp at Les Milles and Allauch, where my family had sought refuge, weren't far way. I didn't have the courage to go to the camp; that was still too much for me. On the other hand, I did go to Allauch, where the old quarter is like a very small, quite charming village in Provence. The château of Carlevent is just outside. It houses some official body or other. I didn't go in, but from the outside it looked spacious and was surrounded by a large garden. I started to imagine my family living in such a place.

When I got back to Paris, I rang my mother to tell her about my visit to Allauch and the castle.

'You know, we lived in Allauch, in the castle,' she told me.

'Why did you think I went there? I knew you'd lived there.'

'How did you find out?'

'Thanks to some documents I've found.'

And she began to tell me how Fritz's cousins, the Wolf family, lived there, that she went to the village school for almost a year and that the inhabitants of Allauch had been kind people because they had tried to hide them.

That's how it is with my mother. I have to find things out first by myself before she'll tell me how they occurred. Then slowly she will let some memories emerge, but only selectively.

Sometimes, it's the other way round and I'm the one who tells her the rest of the story: the part she could not know, which is the cause of so much pain.

25

Some Irrefutable Facts

L'Oréal reckons that it is not responsible for what might have happened before 1961. It is the weightiest argument the multinational deploys to oppose our action. Now that I have in my possession all the documents which prove quite the opposite, dated and stamped by the relevant administrative offices, I will remind you of the following facts:

• The same man, Mr André Tondu, bought Wendstrasse 17, then Wendstrasse 19 and Kaiserallee 18.

• Although he bought Wendstrasse 17 in the name of Ensa Ltd, L'Oréal is the company based at this address. Additionally, Ensa and L'Oréal pursue the same activity: perfumes.

• Mr Tondu bought Wendstrasse 17 in February 1949. He didn't pay cash but took out a loan. Now in Germany, as in most countries, it takes two to four months to get a loan, which means that the promise to sell must have been signed at the end of 1948.

• This same Wendstrasse 17 was acquired in a very strange fashion: two bills of purchase in succession for the same property. The two bills are similar and mention the same buyer and vendors. As if the only real requirement was to alter the date of sale.

• Now this second bill of sale was published in the land registry on 5 November 1951, that is the very same day when BGV signed with the Jewish organization an agreement to ratify the theft of Wendstrasse 19.

Moreover, if Messrs Owen-Jones, Veil and Zaoui have a free moment, they should dip into the archives at the Ministry for Finance and the Economy. And ask to see the file giving information on foreign companies created before 1948 with the help of French capital. There they will see, in black and white, that Haarfarben und Parfümerien has been controlled *100 per cent* since its creation in 1930 by a French firm: *L'Oréal of Paris, 14 rue Royale*[75].

This sequence of anomalies and coincidences should be enough to arouse the suspicions of the most simple-minded among us. How is it possible, from this point on, not to see anything here but the premeditated perpetration of an obscene fraud in order to bypass measures to restore a Jewish property after the war to its rightful owners? Would any of that have been possible if L'Oréal and BGV hadn't colluded?

Wendstrasse 19 couldn't have been sold before 1948 because our property was subject to military government legislation and to measures related to thefts. The first bill of sale for Wendstrasse 17 – in February 1949 – was followed by a complicated administrative process for the purchase of number 19. The presence of my great-uncle Karl didn't make matters any easier: he was cut off from his inheritance in 1951 by the 'agreement' reached between the Jewish organization and BGV.

After 1951 L'Oréal still had to bide its time before it could get its hands on our property: the necessary paperwork at the company registry, the payments of taxes etc. were dealt with in a day. And, in 1953, André Tondu reappears in the property registry, this time to purchase Wendstrasse 19: something that won't happen till the following year.

The past caught up with me as I started on the last part of my story. I had just been called by the person within the Drai Commission responsible for researching my file on what happened at 6 rue des Saussaies[76]. I was really upset by what she told me after my recent reading of the books by the Frydman brothers.

---

75 See Appendices 10 and 11.

76 The study group on the stealing of property belonging to French Jews (the Matteoli Commission) was subsequently replaced by the Drai Commission.

We had been trying to find out the identity of a man my grandfather received in his apartment in Paris, opposite the Ministry of the Interior, 11 rue des Saussaies.

My grandfather's manuscript mentions that it is a diplomat he is well acquainted with. He met him when he was a lawyer working for the French consulate in Karlsruhe. He writes in detail of this diplomat, giving the exact dates of their meetings in the consulate, but never gives his name. This man whom he subsequently welcomed into his home in Paris then occupied an elevated position at the Ministry of the Interior. We wondered whether this unknown individual hadn't played a role in our case. Perhaps he'd just told the people around him of the masterpieces on the walls of Rosenfelders' Paris apartment. He had certainly visited their private townhouse in Karlsruhe.

We hadn't found anywhere documents that mentioned the paintings in my grandparents' Paris home. They had all simply disappeared. Moreover, according to a senior person at the National Archives, there were 'some bizarre things' in our file: it wasn't like most of the 8,000 dossiers checked by the Drai Commission. Consequently – and I wasn't the one who said this – everything pointed to the fact that someone in a high place who knew my grandfather had intervened at the rue des Saussaies before the Gestapo and the Vichy authorities and made a clean sweep of what was in the apartment and, in particular, the paintings.

The woman in charge of research told me of the list of French consuls in Karlsruhe where it appears that a certain Henri Guérin held this position from 1929 to 1936. She advised me to go to the Ministry for Foreign Affairs in order to find out more about this man. No sooner said than done. My heart thudded as I read his file. I won't comment exhaustively on everything I read. What stuck in my mind was how close Henri Guérin was to the powers-that-be, as evidenced by his frequent correspondence with Laval and Pétain among others. In 1939, when he had been living in retirement in Paris from 1936, he indicates to Marshal Pétain that he is at his disposal; and the Marshal writes to him in October 1939 that he wants him to go to Seville and resume his responsibilities.

Moreover, there is one name that keeps cropping up throughout Guérin's career: Camille Chautemps. Guérin owes to the latter all his promotions from the start of his career: 'my close collaborator', 'a personal request from Camille Chautemps', 'collaborator and friend of Camille Chautemps' are the terms used to support Guérin's rise. Whether they come directly from Chautemps or members of ministerial offices – several documents are on Ministry of the Interior stationery – they show the close links between the two men. I didn't know who Camille Chautemps was, and when I returned home I discovered that he was a highly influential man of politics who worked for Pétain to take power.

As chair of the Council of Ministers from February 1930, he saw his second government fall in 1934 after the Stavisky affair. He was a minister for Léon Blum from June 1936 to June 1937 and succeeded him as head of government from June 1937 to March 1938. From 1938 to 1940, he was vice-chair of the Council of Ministers in the Daladier and then the Paul Raynaud governments. From July 1940, he supported the taking of power by Marshal Pétain and formed part of his administration. In November 1940 he left to be ambassador in Washington. He was tried after the war for his acts of collaboration.

My recent reading has also confirmed that *cagoulards* actively supported Pétain's rise to power and that he had in his cabinet men like Gabriel Jeantet, who was close to Eugène Schueller. In this way, the Parisian *cagoulards* (Deloncle, Corrèze, Filliol, Schueller, Lavigne-Deville, Harispe, Duseigneur) had a bridgehead to Vichy (Jeantet, Martin, Méténier, Goussard) and rubbed shoulders with those in power[77].

In terms of my family history, when I read that Corrèze and Deloncle lived in the same apartment at 2 rue Rodin in Paris[78], the address reminded me of something else. And it was in the documents lodged at the company registry in Karlsruhe that I had come across the address of Henri Fèbvre, the L'Oréal lawyer, who acted as proxy for the associates of Haarfarben und Perfümerien (including Liliane Bettencourt), who was a L'Oréal shareholder and close collaborator of Eugène Schueller from 1936: he was based at 4 rue Rodin.

---

77 Pierre Péan, *Le Mystérieux Docteur Martín*, Paris, Fayard,1993, p. 205.

78 Christian Bernadac, *Dagore: Les Carnets secrets de la Cagoule*, Paris, France-Empire, 1977, p. 20.

I wouldn't like my reader to think that I had lost my way and forgotten Henri Guérin *en route*. I have tried to show through this historical section that my research hasn't been linear; I've had to look in several directions at the same time while documenting for myself a period of French history. I've often followed several wrong leads. In the event, Henri Guérin wasn't the man my grandfather saw and that would soon become very clear to me.

I even made the mistake of looking for a consul when his manuscript mentioned a consular attaché. But yet again this mistake was providential. If I hadn't set my research officer on the track of consuls, or begun to take an interest in Guérin, I would probably never have found out the identity of the person we were looking for. In fact, the Ministry for Foreign Affairs could never have supplied us with information on consular attachés: it doesn't have any.

In order to pursue my research, I only had the names of Guérin and Chautemps as clues, as well as what my grandfather had noted in his manuscript about the person he received on the rue des Saussaies who held an important position at the Ministry of the Interior. So I decided to go to this ministry. The archivists at the Ministry of the Interior proved to be very cooperative and efficient. They pointed me to the Fontainebleau Archives that held the documents restored by the Russians – they took them from the Germans who had in turn taken them from France in 1941. They were General Information archives. Perhaps I might glean something yonder.

I went to the Fontainebleau Archives. There were handwritten documents from my grandfather. It was moving to see his handwriting. In perfect French he asked to remain in France; he gave the names of people who would endorse him, including a M. Eugène Faller. There were also letters from police headquarters, from the French Consulate in Karlsruhe, from Renseignements Généraux (an information department of the French police) and handwritten documents from Faller, notably a pass to allow him to visit him at the Ministry of the Interior. Eugène Faller notes there how he had met my grandfather in Karlsruhe where the latter 'was very favourably thought of at the consulate' where Faller had been 'the attaché from 1930'. We had finally found the man we had been looking for. He also worked under the orders of Chautemps (he was an aide to the Chair of the Council of Ministers office, then Secretary of State at the Ministry of the Interior.)

Back home, I studied these documents that I had photocopied. Police headquarters seemed to know everything about my grandfather, his wife and their daughter. It mentions that he owned a large house in Karlsruhe (the address is supplied) and that he was wealthy (this statement is underlined). The information came from the consulate in Karlruhe. What role had this Mr Faller played? Wasn't he my grandfather's friend? It is true the latter speaks of his great disappointment in this respect.

I pursued my enquiries in the Library of the History of Paris at the Town Hall. I discovered a file with Faller's name, with his date, place of birth and other information. He was Prefect several times, worked at the Ministry of the Interior and was promoted time and again during the Occupation. I experienced a feeling of unease and began to understand why my grandfather had been disappointed.

Subsequently, I had access to files of the Prefecture at the National Archives. The 1935–1946 files are headed: 'French Republic, Ministry of the Interior', and then everything is in German. The Faller file was in the same volume as the arch-collaborator Papon's. The latter receives barely more praise than Faller from the Germans. It is recorded that Eugène Faller carries out all their requests most efficiently and compliantly and that he is well connected in French society and in Vichy, that he collaborates with the *Propagandastaffel* and more besides. If I harboured any doubts about the fact that Faller had been a collaborator, now I had none. I also discovered that after the war he remained attached to the civil service without pay for several years, as was common practice with high-ranking civil servants who had a record of collaboration with the Nazis.

I still don't know the precise role that Faller played in the theft of our house, even though I felt there was something amiss. The day after the day in 1937 when my grandfather assigned the powers of attorney in the German Embassy in Paris, he obtained permission for his family to come and stay[79]. It is quite clear: the lives of my great-grandmother, grandmother

79 See Appendices 3 and 4.

and mother were granted in exchange for these powers. It was all well orchestrated by French and German senior civil servants, since my female ancestors got authorization simultaneously to leave Germany and join my grandfather in Paris. Did Faller play an intermediary role between the German authorities and French police headquarters?

Soon afterwards I discovered that there was a file on Faller at the Ministry of the Interior. But in order to consult it I required special authorization, which I was refused. To get it, you had to be related to the person whose file you wanted to see. The refusal letter really annoyed me. I couldn't see any solution that would help me get what I wanted. But, yet again, luck was on my side.

At the time I was rehearsing *Götterdämmerung* at the Toulouse opera house. A singer friend of mine saw I was in a very bad mood and invited me to go for a drink, and as we chatted about one thing and another, she managed to make me laugh. She then asked why I was in such a foul mood, and I told her about being refused access to a file – she already knew the rest of my story. She asked me a few questions about the person I was interested in, and when I mentioned his name, she burst out laughing.

'My mother's maiden name is Faller,' she told me.

This friend is American, but her family is originally from the Black Forest, like Eugène Faller. She spoke to her family, and they responded: 'If someone in our family has behaved badly, it is our duty to make amends.' And they made a request to consult Eugène Faller's file. I hope to have this document soon.

Soon afterwards, I came across a piece of information in a book that really made me shudder[80]: there was a connection between Allauch, the village where my grandparents were arrested, and La Cagoule: on 14 August, a bomb explosion in Nice put the police on the path of the murderers of Marx Dormoy. They found in the murderer's trouser pockets the name of an activist who lived in Allauch, and they immediately questioned him.

---

80 Philippe Bourdrel, *La Cagoule: 30 ans de complots*, Paris, Marabout, Marabout Université, 1986.

I recalled how Eugène Schueller, the founder of L'Oréal, was the ideologue and financier behind La Cagoule (the CSAR). Was it pure chance that my family, who had sought refuge in Allauch, was persecuted? Or was it related to the fact that La Cagoule had a base in the village? I continue to ask myself this disturbing question.

Subsequently, I contacted the municipality of Allauch. I told my interlocutor in what conditions my family had lived there. He was very moved and gave me the details of people to contact: the former mayor, a regional historian…

One of them had known the Wolfs, my grandfather's cousins, at the château of Carlevent, but he had no recollections of my family. I told him that my mother had been saved by a young girl called Rosette; I thus learned that Rosette died when she was thirty-six and that her brother had been executed by the Germans when they discovered he was in the Resistance. But Rosette had a sister who was still alive. He gave me her details, saying that I could say I was calling on his behalf. Her name was Monique Queirel, she was delighted to speak to me and remembered my mother. She was very moved and so was I. In turn, she gave me the telephone number of her very aged older sister. She also remembered my mother and my grandmother but couldn't tell me anything else.

A few days later she telephoned me: memories were flooding back. She remembered my grandfather, whom they called 'Doctor': he was very tall and very thin, with beautiful blue eyes. She couldn't remember what my grandmother looked like. But she had been at their house when she was arrested, apparently by the gendarmes. They had been looking for my family everywhere. That was all. That was already quite a lot.

I continued to call the two sisters from time to time. I liked to speak to them and find out how they were. One day Monique said she had some photos of my family. She sent them to me. There were photos of my mother when she was very young. She was very beautiful. Others of my great-grandmother and grandmother. None of my grandfather.

26

The End of the Voyage

My mother was seventy-five in July 2003. I went to Brazil so we could celebrate her birthday together. I spent more than a month over there and used the opportunity to see people who could give me an outside opinion on my file on the robbery.

First on my list: representatives of various Jewish organizations. I spoke to them about the house, the successive purchasers and about L'Oréal. I showed them the documentation. They were taken aback and gave me their unqualified support: something to which I was not at all accustomed. They were shocked and agreed to do everything possible to allow the truth to be known. I suddenly felt I was no longer alone.

Subsequently, a friend told me that her brother – a highly placed Brazilian magistrate and really trustworthy – had said he would give his impartial opinion on the file, provided I would accept his conclusion if he found I was in the wrong, if indeed that was what he decided. I met him and explained the case at length. He scrutinized the documents carefully and questioned me. He concluded it was a clear case of fraud and that it couldn't be subject to prescription because the receiving and retention of stolen goods constitute a continuous, indivisible crime.

My mother also told me about their passage to Switzerland at the end of 1942. The fisherman-ferryman they contacted had told them that it was getting more and more dangerous, that the lake was under constant surveillance. Finally, he agreed to ferry them across for a goodly sum of money. That same evening, another ferryman transporting refugees had been caught by the Nazis, and everybody was executed. The man who was to take my family to Switzerland immediately came to see my grandfather: it was too risky and he was opting out. My mother related how her lawyer father then started to plead their case in earnest by arguing that the only day when there wouldn't be any danger was precisely the day after the killings. The Nazis would think that nobody would have the courage to make the crossing after such a massacre. The fisherman was all the more easily persuaded when the money on offer was increased. They managed to cross that same night. They later learned they were the last to reach Switzerland unharmed.

On my return to France, Monique Queirel rang me to suggest I spend a few days with her so I could see the house where my family lived for some time. Consequently, I went to Allauch. Monique came to meet me at the bus station and recognized me immediately, because I looked like my mother. Then we walked slowly along the small streets of the old quarter. The weather was fine. I have always really liked the atmosphere in the small villages of Provence. We finally reached their house. You could see the château of Carlevent, on the top of a small hill. My family had lived there with the Wolf cousins. When the latter left for Mexico, my family stayed in the only hotel in the village.

Soon after, I made the acquaintance of the former mayor, who kindly offered me a book about Allauch. Monique's younger sister, Évelyne, joined us. In the course of our conversation, Évelyne told us she would never forget the day when the gendarmes came to get my grandmother. They shook her violently and kept asking her: 'Where is your daughter? Where is your daughter?'

Astonished, I asked: 'You were there?'

'Yes, both Monique and I were there. One thing is certain: they were only after your grandmother and Edith. Your grandfather was already imprisoned in a camp.'

'But why do you say they were only after my grandmother and my mother?'

'Because at the time other Jews were living in the village, and they only took your family.'

'Perhaps because my family was of German origin,' I suggested.

I knew there had been a round up of foreign Jews in the Marseille region, at about the time my grandmother was arrested. It is true that this roundup affected towns, and not villages, but you never know.

Monique replied: 'There *were* other German Jewish families. They were arrested much later, not even that year. At the time, they only wanted your family. Moreover, the gendarmes first went to the château and spoke to Mr Levi, who lived there. He was Jewish, but they didn't bother him. Then, when they went to get your grandmother from the hotel, they found the Dresen family, who were also German Jews but they didn't arrest them. In fact, your grandmother was in our house. They found her by tailing someone who was coming to warn her that the gendarmes were looking for her. It was evident that they only wanted her and Edith, for nobody else was hassled at this point. Only much later, in 1943 or 1944.'

Évelyne continued: 'The gendarmes shook her, but she didn't say where Edith was. And they took her to the camp at Les Milles.'

Taken aback, I asked her: 'And at the time did people know what would happen to the people imprisoned in the Les Milles camp? They say that at the time people still knew nothing about the deportation camps.'

'That's a lie,' replied Monique. 'Everyone knew the Jews were being brought together in camps and then deported. Those who say differently have got something to hide.'

The more indignant she became, the stronger her Marseille accent grew.

In order to lighten the atmosphere, the ex-mayor told a few jokes, and we laughed. Then I asked him if it would be possible to visit the château. He said he'd go and find out, and off he went.

Soon after, Monique came to tell me: 'Come on! We've got a date in front of the château. He's managed to get the keys!'

After the war, this château became an old people's home, then squatters lived there before it was bought by the municipality. As we walked down the path crossing the park, Monique told me what it was like when my grandparents lived there.

We went in and visited the three floors. There was no electricity but as the weather was very good: we could see even when inside. The place had become rather down-at-heel.

I thought of my family. And of all the different places they had lived. The mountains of Rio, the forest, the sea, Switzerland jostled in my head…

The day after, I looked round the village. My mother had asked me to send her photos of her school. As soon as I saw it, I heard in my head the song my mother had sung me on my last visit to Rio when she spoke to me about this school: '*Maréchal, nous voilà…*' My mother sang it through to the end, then added: 'After that, you were allowed to sit down.'

'Mum, am I dreaming or did you just sing me a song in honour of Marshal Pétain?'

She grimaced, as if she'd just swallowed something bitter.

'We all sang it. I had to be like everyone else, I couldn't stand out too much.'

This village was the last place where she lived with her mother. Even if survival was still difficult by this time, it was still possible to hope everything would be all right.

I saw the Mirador Hotel, which is now the Vesuvio restaurant. In a road farther on, Monique stopped me and pointed to the name: rue Pierre-Queirel. Pierre was her older brother. The village had thus paid homage to a great Resistance fighter who had been executed by the Germans.

'What happened to Pierre?'

'They first took him to Marseille, then to Lyon. We know they tortured him a lot because when they took him a change of clothes, the ones they gave us were torn and covered in blood.'

I suddenly thought he might have been a victim of Klaus Barbie. I didn't know what to say. I couldn't stop myself thinking that people like Pierre, like Monique's family, were the real heroes. They too were betrayed by 'respectable' people. We must never let our memories fade. We must not forget what some have done and the crimes others have committed.

We continued our walk. On each street corner, by each alleyway, I imagined my family had been there before me. I took photos. We telephoned my mother. We drank champagne. I was happy to have met these wonderful people. But also filled with melancholy at the thought of all those who had died. We could never be together. It was quite a strange feeling. But you had to do whatever you could. I preferred to try to be as happy as possible at that particular moment.

27

Memorandum

In April 2003, my lawyer finally received a reply in relation to the suit we had filed in December 2001. The ruling delivered by the examining magistrate, following instructions from the public prosecutor, concluded that there could be no trial, arguing, on the one hand, that the French legal system was not competent to judge on the matter, and on the other, that prescription did in fact exist for the crime of receiving and retaining stolen goods.

I was shocked. Soon after, we decided to appeal against the ruling.

I had already been writing the history of this robbery for several months with a view to publishing a book.

Whatever the law decides in the end – and I expect it to perform its function – it can't change anything in relation to the facts. The opposing party can try to silence the truth. But it will never succeed in overturning history. It can, at best, impose a version that some will pretend to believe, depending on their beliefs or the advantages they hope to extract. But the truth will never be changed.

The courts have been created so people don't take justice into their own hands. There should not be powerful people who are beyond the reach of the law, because as soon as the law shuts its eyes to their misdeeds, everything is possible. Impunity is a privilege that takes us back to the Middle Ages. I am certainly naive if I believe in a system of justice where the arbitrary has no place, but what is a world where only power and money count, where conviction no longer plays a part, and where justice is but a word? I dare affirm that it is a world stripped of meaning, a world that is empty.

The appeal memorandum, drawn up my lawyer in support of our case, emphasizes some authenticated facts:

'[…]the power of attorney granted by Fritz Rosenfelder is signed in *Paris* [81] on 24 May1937, and his signature is authenticated by an officer of the law at the consulate in the presence of two witnesses, one of whom is a representative of the said consulate. Quite clearly the document which lists the persons present does not record the presence of Mrs Dürr, the beneficiary of the power of attorney.'

'Evidence that has come to light after the filing of the suit (French archives taken by the Germans, requisitioned by the Soviets and recently given back by the Russians) show that the day after 24 May 1937, 25 May 1937, Fritz Rosenfelder was granted by *the police authorities in Paris* authorization papers to stay in France.'

'Mrs Dürr, equipped with this mandate, will sign in the name of Fritz Rosenfelder […], in Karlsruhe, on 20 January 1938, the bill of sale of the Rosenfelders' magnificent property situated in Karlsruhe at Wendtstrasse 19 on behalf of the Badischer Gemeinde Versicherung Insurance Company (BGV), a company that exists to this day […]. *The amount accrued has never been paid to the "sellers".*'

'Fritz Rosenfelder was forced to carry out a second bill of sale in Paris after the sale on 20 January 1938 […] It thus appears that, after a purchase is evidently enacted on 20 January 1938, the proxy that Fritz Rosenfelder was forced to grant in Paris on 24 May 1937 served to dispossess him of his property situated in Germany, another was enacted in Paris. Thus *two actions to extort*

---

81 Author's emphasis.

signatures were committed in Paris with a clear awareness that these would be used in Germany.'

'The BGV company that "buys" this property on 20 January 1938 keeps it till 1954, the date at which it sells it on to the Haarfarben company represented by its managing director, the French citizen André Tondu. *It has kept ever since the amount it received on this occasion*[…]'

'We have learned after filing our suit that, in respect of the French authorities (a document from the Ministry of Finance and Industry), but not of the German authorities (there is no mention thereof in the Karlsruhe company register), *L'Oréal had a 100 per cent holding in the shares of Haarfarben*; this fact was also known within the enterprise as is evidenced by the CAP papers from the 1947–48 joint production committee of L'Oréal where the actions of André Tondu are specifically celebrated.'

The appeal memorandum addresses the two reasons forwarded by the court of first instance in order not to open the case ('not to proceed'). My lawyer appealed against this decision. He responded in great detail, supporting himself by reference to 'jurisprudence tradition', to articles in the Penal Code, by recalling the way events were interconnected. I won't inflict upon the reader this long legal deliberation. A few sentences will suffice for even a novice to understand that there are no grounds to reject the suit.

The French courts were not competent? Well, 'the competence of the examining magistrate derives from the fact that elements constituting an infringement of the law took place in France', and this is clearly the case in respect of:
- The extortion of my grandfather's signature.
- The instruction given for the purchase of the stolen property.
- The retention, in France, by L'Oréal, of all or part of the proceeds of the stolen property, in other words, theft, by virtue of holding on to the financial gain accruing from this sale.

Could such acts be prescribed? The suit does not focus directly on 'the extorting of a signature', but on the receiving of the product that accrued from this extortion. Thus, 'the extortion of the signature belongs to the category of crimes of the moment, whereas the receiving of stolen goods belongs to the category of continuous crimes.' In this case, 'prescription' only begins to operate from the day when the holding – or profit – has ceased', which is, of course, not the case since the sum accruing from the sale of the house has never been paid to my mother.

Moreover, alongside the supporting evidence, the appeal memorandum demonstrates that 'the L'Oréal group continues [...] to profit from the income from a property the source of which it has always known to be fraudulent.'

In recent years, both in France and Europe, after the official recognition by the President of the French Republic of the responsibility of the French state in relation to the fate that befell Jews, there has been a considerable change of attitude in relation to the theft of Jewish goods in the Nazi era. Different companies have been publicly approached by Jews who, like us, have demonstrated, with supporting proof, that their family had been robbed. Most of these enterprises have apologized, and agreements have been reached to make reparations for the damage caused. They have not tried to shirk their responsibilities, no more than they have tried to shelter behind any pretence of prescription.

I love giving presents. The offering of gifts is one of the most beautiful things in life. But I choose to whom I give presents. Neither the BGV insurance company – apart from its Nazi past, it has held on to the war compensation my mother should have received – nor the Versorgung des Bundes und der Länder (the German State), nor L'Oréal and the Bettencourt couple deserve presents from me!

I am writing this at the end of January 2004. I have just learned that our appeal has been rejected, confirming the conclusions of the public prosecutor: 'outside the competencies of a French presiding magistrate'.

I am not surprised: I have already been told that the court of appeal very rarely contradicts the court of first instance. Now, it has to go to the

Supreme . This decides only on the basis of the application of the law. My lawyer has already made contact with one of his colleagues, *maître* Charles Choucroy, a specialist in appeals to the Supreme Court. And if that is not enough, there is always the European Court of Human Rights. When I think of my mother, of all her suffering and of my decimated family, I tell myself that in any case I have no right to opt out.

For a long time I have wondered: 'Why us?' Why has this family, my family, apparently without a history, inherited such a fate? Moreover, I find it very difficult to accept that I should continue to share its fate. It is because we are Jews that what I have recorded has happened. I do not forget for one moment all those, be they Jewish or not, who suffer a fate similar to ours.

I should never have been able to discover the truth about my family, but deep within me a voice whispers that if I have, it is because life appears to be stronger than all the blankets some individuals would like to use to smother it. I only hope justice can emulate life.

Afterword for the English Edition

Pressure

I had finished the book. At least that is what I thought. I had to start preparing two operas in succession at the Bastille and was immersed in work. Nonetheless, I also needed a lot of time to correct my book in line with requests from my French publisher's lawyers. Words, sentences, turns of phrase had to be changed, and then more and yet more. I had to avoid the slightest possibility that they could accuse me of libel.

At the end of June I decided to go to Brazil and spend a few weeks with my family. The book was finally at the printers. Just before I left, the magazine *Challenger* announced my book would be published in September. This news must have triggered a number of more or less hidden chain reactions, and e-mails from my publisher kept me partly abreast of what was happening. The fact is that by the time of my return to Paris in August, he had decided not to send out extracts from the book before it was published.

It came out, was sent to the newspapers, and I was bombarded by requests for interviews. I was very pleased: the case was finally going to go public. Every journalist who contacted me said he had been convinced by the book's arguments, wanted to be the first to go into print on the subject and assured me that an article would appear in the next issue of his newspaper.

The interviews took place...the articles never appeared. What was wrong? Was pressure being put on the press to stop them from appearing? It was strange: so many requests for conversations that ended in silence.

By then only *Actualités juives* had published a long article. In the two months following its publication, I continued to give a large number of interviews that led to no better outcome than before. I was then contacted by *Le Parisien*. This time an article did appear, on 25 September 2004, revealing that my case would go to the Supreme Court on 12 October. This article also quoted remarks from *maître* Jean Veil, one of L'Oréal's lawyers, stating that all this 'was ridiculous'. It reminded me of gossip that friends had mentioned to me: apparently the rumour was going the rounds that I was 'raving'.

After the article in *Le Parisien*, requests for interviews kept coming in, but with no better results. A woman friend then suggested acting as an intermediary in order to make contact with the presenter of an important television programme. The day before our meeting, *maître* Michel Zaoui, L'Oréal's lawyer, rang my friend to dissuade her from helping me. Their conversation lasted three quarters of an hour. How did *maître* Zaoui find out that my friend had agreed to help me? Apart from my lawyer and myself, no one knew who my intermediary was. My publisher and press officer had been informed of the meeting with the programme producer, but not of my contact's identity. I then felt very acutely the power of L'Oréal and its representatives when it came to finding out information – and felt very uneasy as I imagined this huge network of hidden complicities. How could I struggle, get recognition for the rights of my family, in such conditions? *Maître* Zaoui even knew – he'd mentioned it to my friend – that my own lawyer had arranged a time to meet with a Jewish institution. He knew both the date and time. Yet only my lawyer and I held this information.

It is true that L'Oréal is one of the biggest advertisers in France, that lots of the media need this advertising manna, but I thought naively that in the country of Human Rights, an ethical attitude to news would triumph over any other consideration.

I had to change my tune. More interviews…still no articles. A few journalists were polite enough to tell me of the difficulties they were experiencing in getting their articles into print but could state nothing in public. And at the same time, although I was aware of lots of things, I couldn't say anything either without risking that I myself might be sued for libel.

A few days before 12 October, the date of the hearing of the appeal at the Supreme Court, requests for interviews came fast and furious: for the eight o'clock news on France 2, for I-télé, for France info, France inter… On this occasion, the radio channels did broadcast the interviews with me: on 12 October.

My lawyer and I went to the Supreme Court. I was extremely nervous. There were lots of journalists. Louis di Gardia, the chief public prosecutor at the court, spoke and said that the law as it stood did allow a connection to be established between the extortion of my grandfather's signature, committed in France, and the theft of property that took place on German soil. Consequently, a judge who was competent to try the first crime would be able to pursue the second according to the present jurisprudence of the court.

I got the impression that he had carried out significant research and had plumbed to a deeper level legally, and consequently I was optimistic. While he spoke, tears came to my eyes. I told myself that finally the prejudice suffered by my family would be recognized, that all these years of denials would soon be a thing of the past. I thought particularly of my mother. Our right had been recognized by the most important public prosecutors in the French legal system.

Louis di Gardia made it clear that the signature extorted from my grandfather had been in exchange for the right given to his family to leave Nazi Germany and come to live in France – so that their lives would not be under threat. Louis di Gardia concluded by demanding firstly that the decision of the Court of Paris to reject French legal competency should be revoked, and secondly that the case be opened, on an understanding that the extortion of the signature and stealing of our house were interconnected. We were then informed that the appeal would be heard on 9 November.

That evening, my lawyer and I featured on the eight o'clock news. The telephone went on ringing till very late; I even felt able to answer all the calls. My mother was delighted; she even said she could now start to feel happy. I also immediately sensed that life would never be the same. I suddenly felt fine. Well, just the same as everybody else, that is. As if we had suddenly been given the right to exist. When she learned of the date when the Supreme Court would declare its ruling, my mother reminded me that *Kristallnacht*, the massacre of Jews organized by Goebbels and Himmler in Nazi Germany, took place on 9 November 1938. But that didn't sour our optimism.

The day after my lawyer called to alert me to an article in *Le Monde*: a very good, clear article, telling the facts. The journalist recalled how a few months earlier *maître* Veil had stated that this was all quite ridiculous. Now, whatever happened, nobody could accuse us of being spinners of tall stories. We had made considerable progress!

However, I started to grow anxious again. The most diverse people comforted me: how could I doubt the outcome? The court would follow the guidance of the chief public prosecutor: that should be obvious! His arguments were rock solid. The case would be opened! I replied that I was too familiar with the ways of the L'Oréal people…and that powerful people wield lots of power.

Pandora's Box

I had to spend several weeks in Toulouse, where a production of Donizetti's opera *Lucia di Lammermoor* was being restaged. My contract indicated that preparations would continue to 16 November. But I couldn't possibly envisage being away from Paris on 9 November. I had to negotiate: I should finish preparations on the seventh and return to Toulouse on the tenth for the dress rehearsal with piano: namely, a rehearsal with costumes, make-up, lights and technical support but without the orchestra, with the music played by piano.

So I didn't have very long for rehearsals. A fresh problem cropped up every day: some singers fell ill, others hadn't worked out their previous contracts… But nothing undermined my good spirits, and I felt happy in a way I rarely do. I even felt I was another person physically: I suffer seriously from asthma but didn't have a single attack.

Louis di Gardia had restored my confidence in the system of justice.

As soon as I returned to Paris on 8 November, I was yet again in demand for interviews. I was mainly contacted by legal journalists, and they were very positive in their opinions: the Supreme Court would quash the first ruling and the case would be tried.

When I arrived in the courtroom on the ninth, I felt a great unease. On the previous occasion, the Supreme Court judges had looked me straight in the eye as they took their places. This time, I had the impression that they lowered their eyes as soon as I looked at them. I told myself not to be so silly: I was being really childish! And I looked elsewhere.

And the verdict was given. I could not believe my ears! It was as if the chief public prosecutor at the Supreme Court had never spoken, had never asked for the appeal to be endorsed. My lawyer blanched. I myself felt that night had suddenly descended. I couldn't prevent myself from whispering: 'But who can have intervened?' Of course, I would never get an answer to that question. And even if I did, no interference was necessary: the judges quite simply preferred not to open Pandora's Box.

We should bear in mind that if collaboration began officially in 1940, when the Nazis arrived in France, Eugène Schueller had been actively supporting Nazi ideology from 1935 and had behaved in like fashion. And that from 1937, civil servants in the Ministry of the Interior and Prefecture of Police had straightforwardly collaborated with the German government so the abject exchange of our home could be expedited in return for a residence permit for members of my family who had stayed in Germany so they could live safely in France. They were duped by this agreement since it didn't even save their lives.

France had to wait fifty years to hear the voice of Jacques Chirac recognize its responsibility in the persecution of Jews under the Vichy regime. The country forgot, however, that some people started collaborating well before. The sores are still running, and they try to conceal them. For appearance's sake! L'Oréal is the biggest company in France, one of the country's shop windows. People prefer their shop windows clean. Nevertheless, L'Oréal's dark past is no longer a secret. But money…and power…

I had already heard the two arguments given by the court in order to throw out our appeal: the territorial incompetence of the French judiciary and prescription. Nonetheless, Louis di Gardia, the chief public prosecutor, had demonstrated very clearly before the Supreme Court that there was no basis in law for either.

This is what I call deception. The 'new jurisprudence' breaks totally with legal precedent, and my lawyers were unfairly deprived of the opportunity to voice their opposition: neither the report drawn up by Counsellor Vallat, the recorder at the Supreme Court, nor the address given by Louis di Gardia could lead one to anticipate the court's final ruling. Hypocrisy goes hand in hand with deception: before 1995, France hadn't officially recognized its responsibility in the persecution of the Jews by the Vichy government. Then in 1995 France finally recognized its responsibility. Yet, in the ensuing months, when a case should have been opened, the French justice system concluded it was too late! Before 1995, it was too soon; after, it was too late. France doesn't want to clean its doorstep. It prefers to lecture others.

I had the feeling I no longer existed. As if the refusal to open our case were a sentence against us. They were sentencing my mother to live eternally with the Holocaust, while the family and company of the people presumed responsible for these sufferings had managed to bury the case.

As I left, journalists fired questions at me. I was tremendously disappointed. I made a statement that came straight from the heart: 'We are unimportant, and the L'Oréal people are very important. I really wonder whether France is the country of Human Rights or the country of rights for those who have money and power!'

I felt that some of the journalists were shocked, or at least moved by what had just happened. They were very kind towards me. Some said don't let it stop here, take it to the European Court of Human Rights, don't let things stay as they are. At the time, I didn't know what to think: I had completely lost my confidence in the legal system.

I had to go home, pack my suitcase and catch the plane to Toulouse. But hours passed by, and I couldn't move. Friends kept ringing, but I was like a spectre. My whole body was in pain, and I felt I was living a nightmare. I decided to leave very early in the morning: I wasn't in a fit state to travel. As I closed my eyes, I recalled the words of the president of the court, and it was the face of Captain Dreyfus that came to me.

Support

In Toulouse I had to be straight back on my feet. I had to direct a hundred colleagues in an opera. From time to time someone in the choir or in the technical team would say: 'You're the only person on the radio and telly at the moment.' Some journalists had recorded my reaction on leaving the Supreme Court and had broadcast it. My spirits were raised by the people who came and said: 'Don't let it drop, you must continue.'

When I told my mother of the outcome, she also asked: 'Is there any other way out of this?'

'Yes, there is the European Court of Human Rights.'

'Well, we must concentrate on the European Court, as long as there is a way out, there's hope.'

It is at moments like this that I understand how she could have survived an experience like the Holocaust. I knew she had taken it very badly, but as far as she was concerned, we had to go on. We owed it to all those who were no longer there.

In the days that followed, more and more telephone calls and e-mails urging me to carry on. But where was I going to find the strength to continue? I had no energy left. And what was worse, I had lost one very important ally: the belief I had held till then that justice exists. This was what shocked me most. I had lived my whole life believing in values like honesty, justice and so on. How could I continue to resist if I no longer believed in them?

I needed time to gather my strength. Work was a big help: I had to get things moving. The music brought more consolation than ever before, and I was working with very talented people, people with convictions, and you could feel that in their commitment. But nights were very difficult. I got endless calls. From Brazil, from Paris, from Toulouse, from everywhere. People knew I was very fragile and didn't leave me alone for very long.

When I returned to Paris, e-mails and messages of support were waiting for me, and some suggested setting up a support committee. Members of the Culture Commission of B'nai Brith said they wanted to be behind the support committee; a website was started, and more than a thousand signatures were collected in two weeks, it still operates today: http://www.lorealapris.com

Poison

For its part, L'Oréal went back on the offensive. In an article that appeared in an American magazine, *Christian Science Monitor*, L'Oréal states that 'the family has already been compensated'. Always the same old tune to make us sound as if we were dishonest! With variations: sometimes, the house purchase had been settled before the war; at others, the settlement was agreed by a Jewish association after the war. We should spell things out clearly.

There were in effect Jews who were forced to sell their property and who received a derisory payment in the Nazi era. Nevertheless, in such cases, the tribunals have always ruled that this property was stolen, and compensation has been paid. Now my family was paid nothing at all in the Nazi era. *Rien du tout*! Zero! *Niente*! *Nada*! Nothing!

As for the Jewish institution that we have already discussed in this book, things are also quite clear. Except that this implies that Jews were themselves responsible for the robbery: a contemptible subtext. Of course, L'Oréal is never to blame!

The Jewish organization that was indeed contacted after the war had taken care to indicate, in article three of the agreement reached with BGV, that if the previous rightful owners presented themselves, the agreement would be rendered null and void[82]. The fact is we are here. The family is the one my mother was able to create, and that was after the robbery. I was born at the end of 1953 and my brother in 1952. We are the rightful owners – everybody else is dead – and none of us has ever received anything. *Ever*.

With hindsight, one might think that this association should have undertaken the search for the rightful owners. But we ought to point out that this association was acting in an emergency situation to try to resolve all the problems flowing from the Holocaust in Germany. People who had

82 See the agreement, Appendix 8.

disappeared, survivors without resources, property that had been stolen…
And at the time there was no fax or Internet; even the telephone wasn't so
common. Only six months! Hence, the precaution taken in article three of
the agreement, so that possible lawful owners could recover what was
owed to them. L'Oréal bought my family's house in full knowledge of all
of this. Because I don't think it was a chance thing that my mother found
it so difficult to get hold of documents concerning the ownership of the
house over all these years. I also recall that their contract of purchase
explicitly noted that it was a stolen house[83].

In any case, today L'Oréal can no longer plead ignorance to these facts:
that this house belonged to us, that its pseudo-sale is the result of blackmail
and that reparations have never been made for this theft. L'Oréal
nevertheless still continues at every point to search for excuses to avoid
accepting its responsibilities. That is what I find most shameful. Rather
than trying to find a human solution, they do everything to leave us out
of account.

The only truth is that this house was stolen from us during Nazi rule
because we are Jewish. And 'the family', as they say, the family no longer
exists. They are dead. Only their descendants remain: we, the lawful
owners.

L'Oréal prevents us from turning the page, from regaining our peace of
mind, from letting all those who did not return rest in peace.

It is no use at all saying 'Never again!' and refusing to settle the dramas of
the past. Problems aren't settled by speeches. But by deeds.

Europe was the cradle for all this barbarism. It has a duty to look its past
in the face if it is to build its future and realize promises of a Europe at peace
with itself and with others. This peace can only come with justice.

That is what I now expect from the European Court of Human Rights.

---

83 See Appendix 6.

Epilogue

CENTRAL CONSISTORY
Union of Jewish Communities of France
The President

Paris, 9 November 2005

Madame Monica WEITZFELDER
2, Place Charles Bernard
75018 PARIS

Dear Monica,

I would like to confirm via this letter that I am completely in support of the case you are fighting in order to recover the building situated in Karlsruhe and which was acquired at a time when the arrangements were not really clear by the L'Oréal Company situated in Clichy, near Paris.

I not only confirm that I am completely in support of your just cause but that I am ready to contact L'Oréal or other third parties to help you in this process.

Please keep me informed of the stage reached by your researches and procedure and, dear Monica, be assured of my continued interest in this matter.

Yours faithfully
Jean Kahn

Appendices

Chronology

1930. André Tondu is mandated by Eugène Schueller to found Haarfarben und Parfümerien GmbH in Berlin.

24 May 1937. Power of attorney signed in Paris under constraint by Fritz Rosenfelder in favour of Mrs Luise Dürr.

25 May 1937. Paris Prefecture grants permission to stay to Fritz Rosenfelder and to bring his family to France.

January 1938. The house at Wendstrasse 19 passes into the hands of the Badischer Gemeinde Versicherung Verband (BGV).

1945. André Tondu, mandated by Eugène Schueller, transfers Haarfarben und Parfümerien GmbH to Karlsruhe (L'Oréal Germany whose head office was 14 rue Royale, Paris).

1 January 1949. End of administrative restrictions imposed by the Allies on Jewish property stolen by the Nazis.

February 1949. André Tondu, director of Ensa, and representing Eugène Schueller for Haarfarben und Parfümerien GmbH (L'Oréal Germany), buys from Mrs Pfeiffer the building at Wendstrasse 17, adjacent to Wendstrasse 19.

5 November 1951. New bill of sale for the same Wendstrasse 17, between Mrs Pfeiffer and André Tondu for Ensa (still representing Haarfarben und Parfümerien GmbH, L'Oréal Germany). The same day BGV and a Jewish association, the JRSO, reach an agreement on Wendstrasse 19, without contacting Edith Rosenfelder-Waitzfelder and Karl Rosenfelder. Also that same day André Tondu, on behalf of

Haarfarben und Parfümerien GmbH (L'Oréal Germany), buys Kaiserallee 18, also adjacent to our house at Wendstrasse 19.

1954. BGV sells our house, Wendstrasse 19, to Haarfarben und Parfümerien GmbH (L'Oréal Germany). The bill of sale indicates that the house was property stolen in the Nazi era.

May 1991. The Frydman affair becomes public knowledge; the dark years of L'Oréal come to the surface.

June 1991. L'Oréal sells Wendstrasse 19 (our house) to the Versorgung des Bundes und der Länder.

Spring 2000. Copy of the land registry deeds of Karlsruhe sent to the Rosenfelder-Waitzfelder family.

June 18 2001. Our lawyer, *Maître* Korman, informs L'Oréal that the heir Edith Rosenfelder-Waitzfelder requests the return of the property stolen from her.

June 2001. Our lawyer, *Maître* Korman informs BGV and the Versorgung des Bundes und der Länder that the heir Edith Rosenfelder-Waitzfelder requests the return of the property stolen from her.

12 July 2001. First reply from Mr Owen-Jones on behalf of L'Oréal.

August 2001. Replies from the BGV and from the Versorgung des Bundes und der Länder.

28 December 2001. *Maître* Korman files a suit against theft in the name of his client, Edith Rosenfelder-Waitzfelder.

March 2006. L'Oréal buys the British Body Shop chain for £652 million (€940 million)

The **ROSENFELDER-WAITZFELDER** Family

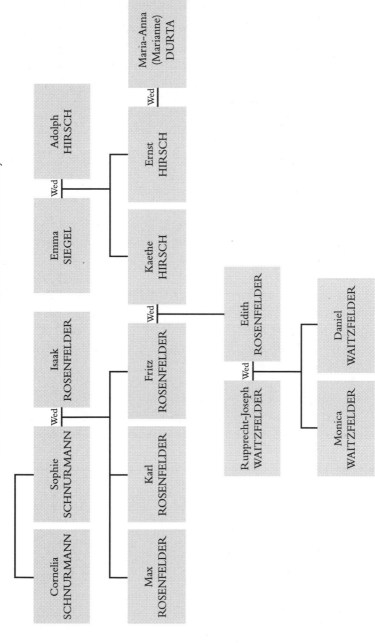

Copy of the Title Deeds in the Karlsruhe Property Registry

The name Rosenfelder is clearly legible.

Haarfarben und Parfümerien, Gesellschaft mit beschränkter Haftung in Karlsruhe.

Aufgelassen am 9.Juni
1954 und eingetragen am
23.September 1954.(AS...)

4

Translation

Entry	Owner	Date and reason for purchase	Value
1.	2.	3.	4.
		Entry in old Title Deeds	Purchase Price 26,600 Marks
1.	KIRCHENBAUER [Illegible]	Volume 90, page 918,n° 123 31 March 1900, (A.S.$^{1}/_{4}$)t	Suppl. Fire Insurance: 59,000 Marks 108.100 Marks
2.	Sofia, maiden name SCHURNMANN, Widow of the private individual Isaak ROSENFELDER here	entry listed 2 April 1919 and re-entered 9 May 1919 (A.S:141//158)	Valued by the Court 19 April 1901: 88,000 Marks (A.S.19) [illegible] 136.000 Marks (cf.A.S.29)
3.	The Badischer Gemeinde – Versicherungs Verband Insurance Company Access blocked! (Section II,Number 4)	entry listed 15 March and re-entered 23 May 1938 (AS 285/86)	Valued by the Court 20 June 1904: 144,000 Marks (AS 71/V) Fiscal value 1907: 9,145,000 Marks
4.	The Haarfarben und Parfümerien, Gesellshaft mit beschränkter Haftung Company (hair colouring products and perfumery articles), Karlsruhe	entry listed 9 June 1954 and re-entered 23 September 1954 (AS 325)	Fiscal value [illegible] 345,800 Marks KV (A.S:163)
	Closed		

Extract from the Entry from the Registry of Births for Edith Rosenfelder, Dated 1952, Sent by the Karlsruhe Town Hall

Geburtsurkunde

(Standesamt Karlsruhe — — — — — — — — Nr. 1354/1923).

— — — Edith Karla R o s e n f e l d e r — — —

ist am 2. Juli 1923 — — — — — — — — — — — — — —

in Karlsruhe — — — — — — — — — — — — — — geboren.

Vater: Doktor der rechte Fritz Rosenfelder, —
Rechtsanwalt, wohnhaft in Karlsruhe — — — — — —

Mutter: Käthe Henriette Rosenfelder, geborene
Hirsch, wohnhaft in Karlsruhe — — — — — — — —

Anderungen der Eintragung:

Karlsruhe den 30. September 2 195..

Der Standesbeamte:

Elisabeth Lichter
Dipl.-Übersetzerin

20.08.1997

The entry doesn't record the death of Edith Rosenfelder, whereas the entry for her mother Kaethe Rosenfelder does record hers.

Letter from Fritz Rosenfelder 22 December 1937

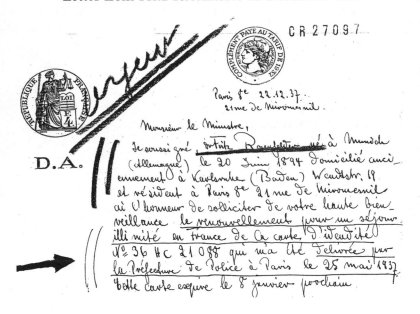

[...]

Fritz Rosenfelder states that he received his residence card, issued by the Police Prefecture in Paris on 25 May 1937, the day after he signed the power of attorney at the German Consulate in Paris.

Translation

Paris 8e. 22.12.37
21 rue de Miromesnil

Dear Minister,

I the undersigned, Dr Fritz Rosenfelder, born in Munich (Germany), 20 June 1894 formerly resident in Karlsruhe (Baden) Wendstr.19 and resident in Paris 8 21 rue de Miromesnil is honoured to request from you <u>the renewal for unlimited stay in France of identity card n° 36 HC 21088 issued by the Police Prefecture in Paris 25 May 1937</u>. This card expires 8 January next

Dr Fritz Rosenfelder

4
Power of Attorney Signed Under Constraint in Paris 24 May at the German Consulate

Piere N°9

G e n e r a l v o l l m a c h t .

Paris, den 24. Mai 1937.))

Ich bestelle hierdurch Frau Luise Dürr, Karlsruhe (Baden), Viktoriastrasse zu meiner Generalbevollmächtigten und ermächtige sie zur Besorgung aller meiner Angelegenheiten.

Sie soll befugt sein, jedes Rechtsgeschäft und jede sonstige Rechtshandlung, welche ich selbst vornehmen könnte, und bei welchen eine Stellvertretung gesetzlich zulässig ist, an meiner Statt und mit derselben Wirkung vorzunehmen, als ob ich die Handlung selbst vorgenommen hätte.

Die Bevollmächtigte soll auch befugt sein, für meine Rechnung Versicherungen jeder Art zu nehmen, allgemeine und besondere Bevollmächtigte jeder Art und zu allen Geschäften zu bestellen sowie auch die Gesamtheit der ihr nach dieser Vollmacht zustehenden Befugnisse auf einen anderen zu übertragen.

Die genannte Generalbevollmächtigte soll alle ihnen vorstehend übertragenen Befugnisse auszuüben befugt sein.

Die vorstehend erteilte Vollmacht soll durch meinen Tod nicht erlöschen.

gez. Dr. Fritz Rosenfelder.))

Verhandelt Paris, den 24. Mai 1937.))

Der dem unterzeichneten Gesandtschaftsrat Dr. Bräutigam durch Vorlage seines Reisepasses Nr. 2503, Polizeipräs. Karlsruhe 8.VII.33/38, ausgewiesene Reichsangehörige Dr. Fritz Rosenfelder, z.Zt. Paris, gegen dessen Verfügungsfähigkeit kein Bedenken obwaltet, legte das vorstehende Schriftstück vor und erklärte mit dem Antrage auf Beglaubigung, dass er die darunter befindliche Unterschrift Dr. Fritz Rosenfelder zum Zeichen der Genehmigung selbst geschrieben habe.

Translation

<u>Copy</u>

<u>Power of attorney</u>

Paris, 24 May 1937

I designate herewith Madame Luise DÜRR, Karlsruhe (Bade), Viktoriastrasse, as my legal representative with full powers of attorney authorising her to deal with all my business.

She is thus authorized to sign any legal paper that I could sign myself and for which the law authorizes her to represent me legally and to act in my name, giving these papers the same validity they would have if I had signed them myself.

My representative is thus equally authorized to contract, on my behalf, in whatever way, to give general or special powers to any legal representative in order to sign any legal act, as well as to transfer all the rights that issue from the present letter to a third person.

The representative designated herewith, having powers of attorney, is authorized to exercise all the above-mentioned rights.

The power of attorney will remain valid after my death.

Signed Dr Fritz Rosenfelder

Made in Paris, 24 May 1937.

The present document was presented to the delegated legal officer signed here below Dr BRÄUTIGAM, on the presentation of passport n° 2508, issued by the *Polizeipräsium* [police headquarters] Karlsruhe 8.VIII.33/38 belonging to the citizen of the Reich Dr Fritz ROSENFELDER, presently living in Paris and in full possession of his legal rights; Dr Fritz ROSENFELDER has stated, when requesting the legalizing of this document, that the signature 'Dr Fritz ROSENFELDER' placed at the end of the document endorsing its approval has been written by his own hand.

5

Bill Ceding the Rosendfelder Property, Wendstrasse 19, to the Badischer Gemeinde Verband (BGV), Issued Under the Nazi Regime

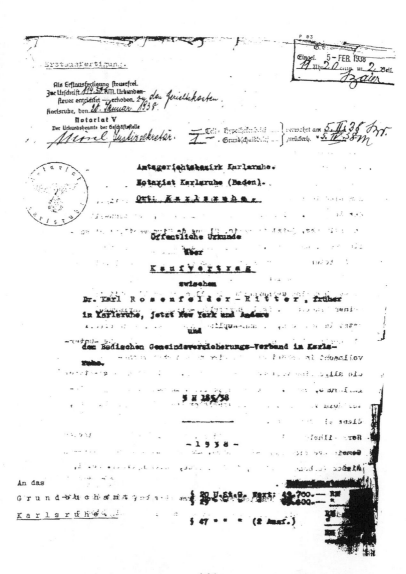

Die Übereinstimmung vorstehender Abschrift mit der vorgelegten und wieder zurückgegebenen Urschrift wird beglaubigt.

Karlsruhe, den 20. Januar 1938.

Notariat 5

Justizrat _(signature)_ ,als Notar.

Last page of the bill of concession to the BGV in 1938 complete with the swastika of the Third Reich.

6

Transfer of the Property on 29 June 1954 from the BGV to Haarfarben, Signed by André Tondu

A u s f e r t i g u n g .

Amtsgerichtsbezirk Karlsruhe

Notariat Karlsruhe (Baden)

Ort: K a r l s r u h e .

Öffentliche Urkunde

über

K a u f v e r t r a g

zwischen

Badischen Gemeindeversicherungsverband, öffentliche
Körperschaft in Karlsruhe

und

Firma Haarfarben und Parfümerien, Gesellschaft
mit beschränkter Haftung in Karlsruhe.

– IV H 789/54 –

– – – – – – – – – – – –

Jahr 1954.

An das
G r u n d b u c h a m t ,
K a r l s r u h e

eingetragen:
Badischer Gemeindeversicherungsverband in Karlsruhe.

Reichsmark-Rechte wurden nach dem 20. Juni 1948 in der III. Abt. nicht gelöscht. Eine Hypothekengewinnabgabe ruht somit auf dem Grundstück nicht. Bezüglich des Eigentums des Grundstücks war ein Rückerstattungsverfahren anhängig, das erledigt wurde, sodaß der derzeitige Eigentümer voll verfügungsberechtigt ist.

[...]

Die Ansprüche aus Kriegssachschaden verbleiben in voller Höhe dem Verkäufer.

[...]

gez. Wilhelm Krause
"   André Tondü
gez. Kammer.

Translation

is registered under the name of:
Badischer Gemeindeversicherungsverband in Karlsruhe.

According to section III, the rights to convert the Reichsmark were registered after 20 June 1948. Consequently, the terrain is free of any tax on profits from the mortgage. A restitution procedure was begun concerning the ownership of this property; the file has been closed, so that the present owner is fully entitled to dispose of the property.

[...]

The compensation rights owed to victims of the war remain entirely within the possession of the vendor.

[...]

Signed Wilhelm KRAUSE
Signed André TONDU
Signed KAMMER

[...]

7

Bill of Sale of the Lot Contiguous to Wendstrasse 19, 25 February 1954 on Behalf of Ensa, Renewed 5 November 1951

- A u s f e r t i g u n g -

Amtsgerichtsbezirk Karlsruhe

Notariat Karlsruhe (Baden)

Ort: K a r l s r u h e

Öffentliche Urkunde

über

A u f l a s s u n g

u.a. zu Kaufvertrag vom 25. Februar 1949

zwischen

der Firma "Ensa G.m.b.H. für Chemie und Kosmetik"in Karlsruhe,

u n d

Frau Lina N a g e l geb. Pfeifer in Karlsruhe.

- I H 2516/51 -

- - - - - - - - - - - -

Jahr 1951.

An das

Grundbuchamt

K a r l s r u h e

170

nebst 6% Zinsen nach näherer Massgabe der oben für das Restkauf-
geld festgelegten Zahlungsbedingungen, zu Gunsten von Frau Lina
Nagel geb. Pfeifer.

S c h l u s s :

Ausfertigungen sollen erhalten:

a) die Beteiligten,

b) das Grundbuchamt Karlsruhe.

Hierüber Urkunde,

auf Vorlesen von den Anwesenden genehmigt und von ihnen und
dem Notar, wie folgt, eigenhändig unterschrieben:

gez. André Tendu

"   Dr. Friedrich Nagel

gez. Deimling, Notar.

- - - - - - - -

Diese Ausfertigung der amtlich zu verwahrenden
Urschrift ist richtig.

Ausgefertigt für das Grundbuchamt

K a r l s r u h e

zum Eintrag gegen Vollzugsanzeige.

Verzichtserklärung des Finanzamtes Karlsruhe vom 21.12.5o ist ange-
schlossen.

Karlsruhe, den 5. November 1951
Notariat I Karlsruhe

Oberjustizrat   als Notar.

Translation

Copy

District of the Court of First Instance of Karlsruhe

Office of the Karlsruhe notary (Baden)

Place: Karlsruhe

Official note

concerning

the entry into the property register

among others concerning the bill of sale of 25 February 1949

between

the company "Ensa Gm.b.H. für Chemie und Kosmetik" at Karlsruhe.

and

Mrs Lina NAGEL, née PFEIFER, at Karlsruhe.

IH 2516/51

Year 1951

A: Property Register
Karlsruhe

as well as 6% interest according to the conditions of payment of the outstanding sum of the purchase price defined above, in favour of Mrs Lina NAGEL, née PFEIFER

Conclusion:

A copy will be sent:

to those party to the contract,
to the Property Registry of Karlsruhe.

Bill established,

Read, approved and personally signed by the persons here present as follows

Signed André TONDU,
Signed Dr Friedrich NAGEL

Signed DEIMLING, notary.

This copy of the original co-signed bill is complete.

Made for the property registry
of Karlsruhe

to be entered on notification of completion.

The statement of waiving of rights from the Ministry of Finance (the treasury office) of Karlsruhe of 21 December 1950 is attached.

Karlsruhe, 5 November 1951*
Notary's Office of Karlsruhe

Legal officer [illegible signature], as notary.
[Stamp of the Karlsruhe notary's office]

[Stamp of the Karlsruhe notary's office]

[handwritten: illegible]

---

* French translator's note: This bill begins with the declaration 'Made in Karlsruhe, 26 October 1951', whereas the date of the signature on the present page is 5 November 1951.

8

Document Concerning the Settlement on 5 November 1951 Between a Jewish Organization and the BGV Authorizing the Latter to Dispose of Wendstrasse 19

Amtsgericht Karlsruhe.   Karlsruhe, den 5.November 51
Schlichter f.Wiedergutmachung

Reg. K (IRSO) 1045

Gegenwärtig:

Landgerichtsrat Hampel   In Sachen
als Schlichter,
                                          der Jewish Restitution Successor Organi-
Justizangestellte Harder   zation, Inc., New.York, (IRSO)
als Urkundsbeamter,
                                                    Antragstellerin -
                                          (Verf.: Dr.Fritz Rosenfelder und Dr.Karl
                                           Rosenfelder-Ritter)

                                                    g e g e n

                                          den Bad.Gemeindevers.Verband-öffentl.
                                          rechtlicherKörperschaft in Karlsruhe
                                                    Antragsgegner

                                          wegen Rückerstattung des Grundstücks
                                          Lgb.Nr. 525 ca,(Wendstr. 19) in Karlsruhe

sind erschienen:

1.) Für die IRSO Herr Dr. R i e d e l aus Mannheim als Allge-
    meinbevollmächtigter der IRSO

2.) für den Antragsgegner Herr Dr. Wilhelm K r a u s e aus
    Karlsruhe, Barbarossaplatz 2,

eine Bestätigung über seine Vertretungsbefugnis vom 21.8.1950
zur Einsicht vorlegend.

Die Beteiligten nahmen Bezug auf die Sitzungsniederschrift v.
26.6.1951 und einigten sich hierauf im Wege des

                              V e r g l e i c h s

gütlich dahin:

1.) Der Antragsgegner verpflichtet sich, an die IRSO zur Abfindung
    deren Ansprüche 5000,— Deutsche Mark umgehend nach Rechts-
    wirksamwerden des Vergleichs zu bezahlen.

2.) Im Hinblick auf diese Zahlung verbleibt der Antragsgegner im
    Eigentum des Grundstücks Wendstr. 19.

3.) Die IRSO verpflichtet sich, den Antragsgegner bis zur Höhe von
    5000,— Deutsche Mark schadlos zu halten, falls sich noch
    Besserberechtigte melden sollten, die den Antragsgegner mit Er-
    folg in Anspruch nehmen, vorausgesetzt, dass der Antragsgegner
    sich den Weisungen der IRSO entsprechend verhält.

4.) Etwaige Ansprüche gegen das frühere Deutsche Reich oder seinen
    Rechtsnachfolger wegen Kriegssachschädenansprüchen verbleiben
    dem Antragsgegner.

5.) Durch diese Einigung sind sämtliche Ansprüche der Beteiligten,
    soweit sie mit dem Erwerb oder Rückgewähr des Grundstücks im
    Zusammenhang stehen, abgegolten.

                                                         ./.

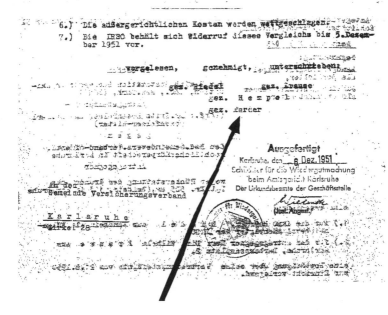

6.) Die außergerichtlichen Kosten werden wettgeschlagen.

7.) Die IRSO behält sich Widerruf dieses Vergleichs bis 5. Dezember 1951 vor.

vorgelesen,   genehmigt,   unterschrieben:

gez. Riedel   gez. Krause

gez. H e m p e l

gez. Karder

Ausgefertigt

Karlsruhe, den 6. Dez. 1951

Schlichter für die Wiedergutmachung beim Amtsgericht Karlsruhe

Der Urkundsbeamte der Geschäftsstelle

(Just. Angest.)

Gemeinde Versicherungsverband

K a r l s r u h e

There is no Rosenfelder signature.

175

Translation

Agreement
Copy

Karlsruhe Court of First Instance   Karlsruhe, 5 November 1951
Negotiator responsible for Reparation Affairs
Rest K (IRSO) 1045

In the presence of:
Mrs Hempel, Member of the High Court
acting as negotiator

Marder, court employer and recorder

In the case opposing
The Jewish Restitution Successor Organization, Inc., New York (JRSO)

– claimants –

(victim of persecution: Dr.Fritz Rosenfelder and Dr. Karl Rosenfelder-Ritter)

to the:

Bad. Gemeindevers. Verband, legally established company, in Karlsruhe

– defendant –

for the restitution of the property entered under land register number 525 a (Wendstr. 19) in Karlsruhe.

there appeared:
1. for the JRSO: Dr. Reidel, from Mannheim, in his position as general agent for the JRSO;
2. for the defendant: Director Wilhelm KRAUSE, residing in Karlsruhe, Barbarosatzplatz   2;
   who presented a statement certifying his capacity to represent, dated 21/08/1950.
   Those present, referring to the minutes of the hearing of 26/06/1951, reached a settlement by means of an

Agreement

as follows:
1. The defendant agrees to pay the JRSO, as soon as the agreement has become legal and binding, the sum of 5000 German marks as compensation.
2. Consequent on this payment, the defendant retains ownership of the land on Wendtstr.19.

3. The JRSO agrees, provided that the defendant acts in accordance with the instructions of the JRSO, to exonerate the defendant to the extent of 5000 DM, if the case arises where the legal owners should make themselves known and validly contest the defendant.
4. The possible rights against the former German Reich, or its successor, in terms of war compensation, fall to the defendant.
5. The present agreement relieves the parties of all their interests in relation to the purchase or restoration of the land.
6. The non-legal expenses will be paid between the parties concerned.
7. The JRSO reserves its right to withdraw from the present settlement to 5 December 1951.

Read, approved and signed:

Riedel   Krause   Hempel   Harder

Agreement reached
in Karlsruhe, 6 December 1951
Negotiator responsible for Reparation Affairs
at the Karlsruhe Court of First Instance
Secretary
[signature]

The settlement is null and void if the legal owners appear as set out in the conditions in clause 3.

9
Letter from Lindsay Owen-Jones 12 July 2001
to Edith Waitzfelder's Lawyer

L'ORÉAL   Clichy, le 12 juillet 2001

M. Charles Korman
Avocat au Barreau de Paris
66, avenue Kléber
75116 Paris

Maître,

La lettre du 18 juin 2001 que vous m'avez adressée à la demande de Mme Edith Rosenfelder, veuve Waitzfelder, a retenu toute mon attention.

Après m'avoir rappelé le sort subi pendant la dernière guerre par la famille Rosenfelder, juifs allemands persécutés par le régime nazi, vous m'exposez que la société que je préside aurait bénéficié d'un avantage indu que vous chiffrez à 60.556.726 DM (soit plus de 200.000.000 FF).

Vous précisez qu'en 1938 les parents de Mme Rosenfelder ont été contraints de vendre un immeuble à la compagnie d'assurances Badischen Gemeindeversicherungsverban. En 1954 (16 ans après la spoliation et 10 ans après la chute du 3ème Reich), la compagnie d'assurance a cédé le terrain nu (l'immeuble ayant été détruit pendant la guerre) à la société Haarfarben und Parfümerien GmbH, filiale allemande de L'Oréal. Cette filiale a acquis le terrain voisin et fait construire sur l'ensemble un immeuble de bureaux. Elle a revendu le tout en 1991. Vous analysez ces faits comme constitutifs d'un recel en France comme en Allemagne. L'Oréal SA aurait, selon votre opinion, commis ce délit du seul fait de sa perception des dividendes versés par sa filiale allemande.

Au-delà des accusations que vous proférez sans aucune réserve et qui me blessent personnellement, la demande que vous formulez sur un ton comminatoire inhabituel pour un avocat suscite de nombreuses questions, tant de fait que de Droit, qui ne sont, ni de pure forme, ni dilatoires.

A défaut de paiement au plus tard le 18 juillet 2001 de la somme de 200 millions de FF, vous m'indiquez avoir d'ores et déjà reçu instruction de déposer, entre les mains de M. le Doyen des juges d'instruction près le Tribunal de grande instance de Paris, une plainte avec constitution de partie civile pour recel d'extorsion de fonds à l'encontre de notre société et de ses filiales.

La Shoah représente pour moi, comme pour toute personne soucieuse des valeurs humaines, la tragédie absolue et ma compassion à l'égard des victimes est totale. Il est légitime que ces dernières demandent réparation, mais cela n'autorise pas à poursuivre sans fondement une personne physique ou morale. Or ma plus grande conviction est que L'Oréal n'a causé aucun tort à Mme Edith Rosenfelder. Aussi, ai-je demandé à vos confrères Michel Zaoui et Jean Veil de nous représenter et de procéder avec vous à une analyse juridiquement incontestable de la situation.

Je vous prie d'agréer, Maître, mes sentiments distingués.

Lindsay OWEN-JONES

Translation

L'ORÉAL

Clichy, 12 July 2001

M.Charles Korman
Lawyer at the Paris Bar
66, avenue Kléber
75116

Maître,

The letter of 18 June 2001 that you sent me concerning the request of Mrs Edith Rosenfelder, widow Waitzfelder, has exercised me greatly.

After reminding me of the fate suffered in the last war by the Rosenfelder family, German Jews persecuted by the Nazi regime, you tell me that the company I head must have benefited from an unwarranted income that you estimate at 605,567,26 DM (or more that 200,000,000 French francs).

You note that in 1938 the parents of Mrs Rosenfelder were forced to sell a property to the Badischen Gemeindeversicherungsverban insurance company. In 1954 (six years after the robbery and ten years after the fall of the Third Reich), the insurance company ceded the empty land (the building having been destroyed in the war) to Haarfarben und Parfümerien GmbH, the German subsidiary of L'Oréal. This subsidiary acquired the neighbouring lot and built an office block on the extended lot. It resold everything in 1991. You analyse these acts as constituting a theft both in France and Germany. L'Oréal would have, in your opinion, committed this crime via the simple act of receiving dividends as paid by its German subsidiary.

Apart the accusations that you make without any reservations whatsoever and which hurt me personally, the demand you formulate in threatening terms unusual for a lawyer suggest numerous questions, in matters of fact and law that are not purely a question of form, or of deferment.

If there is no payment at the latest by 18 July of the sum of 200 million French francs, you indicate that you have been requested forthwith to lodge with the Chief Public Prosecutor in the Paris Court of First Instance a law suit in terms of the receiving, retention and extortion of funds against our company and its subsidiaries.

The Shoah represents for me, as for anyone concerned with human values, an absolute tragedy and my compassion for the victims is unreserved. It is legitimate for the latter to seek reparation, but that gives no authority for the unwarranted pursuit of a physical or moral person. My deepest conviction is that L'Oréal has done no wrong to Mrs Edith Rosenfelder. On this basis, I have requested that your colleagues <u>Michel Zaoui and Jean Veil</u> represent us and proceed with you to a legally irrefutable analysis of the situation.

Yours sincerely,

Lindsay OWEN-JONES

10

Document Obtained from the Ministry of the Economy, Finance and Industry Where One Can Read: 'Haarfarben und Parfümerien GmbH-L'Oréal, Paris, 14 rue Royale – a 100% French company'

ANNEXE VI

RENSEIGNEMENTS PRINCIPAUX PAR ORDRE ALPHABETIQUE
SUR LES SOCIETES ALLEMANDES A PARTICIPATIONS FRANCAISES
CREEES AVANT LE 19 JUIN 1948 (REFORME MONETAIRE)

[...]

HAARFARBEN + U. PARFÜMERIE GmbH   L'OREAL,Paris,14 rue Royale   20.000 100 %
Ber - Steglitz

Translation

APPENDIX VI

PRINCIPAL INFORMATION IN ALPHABETICAL ORDER ON GERMAN COMPANIES WITH FRENCH INVESTMENT CREATED BEFORE <u>19 JUNE 1948</u> (MONETARY REFORM)

[…]

Haarfarben u.Parfumerien GmbH, L'Oréal, Paris, 14 rue Royale 20000 100%

11

Letter from Lindsay Owen-Jones Addressed to Edith Waitzfelder

L'ORÉAL

Clichy, le 4 octobre 2001

Madame Edith Waitzfelder

c/ Me Charles Korman
66, avenue Kléber
75116-Paris

c/ Madame Monica Waitzfelder
2, place Charles Bernard
75018-Paris

Madame,

Me Charles Korman m'a écrit en votre nom le 18 juin 2001 pour attirer mon attention sur votre situation et me demander de faire verser par le groupe que je préside un montant de 60.556.726 DM afin de vous indemniser de la spoliation dont vos parents ont été les victimes du fait du régime nazi.

Comme vous le savez, j'ai demandé à nos avocats de se rapprocher du vôtre pour prendre connaissance du dossier afin de pouvoir m'éclairer.

Je comprends que les faits qui sont à l'origine de cette affaire concernent l'achat en 1938 par une compagnie d'assurance allemande d'un immeuble situé à Karlsruhe en Allemagne et appartenant à vos parents alors citoyens allemands. En 1951, une association juive, légalement désignée pour se substituer aux juifs exterminés par le régime nazi, et votre oncle, rescapé de la Shoah, dont vous êtes l'héritière, ont contesté judiciairement cette acquisition puis ont signé avec la compagnie d'assurance une transaction qui a été homologuée par le Juge allemand des Restitutions, juridiction spécialisée mise en place par les Alliés après la guerre.

En 1954, l'agent de l'Oréal en Allemagne, dont le groupe a racheté les actions en 1961 seulement, a acquis le terrain qui portait les bâtiments détruits par les bombardements. Ce terrain a été intégré dans un ensemble plus vaste, revendu en 1991.

J'ai découvert cette situation à la lecture de la lettre de votre avocat et j'ignorais jusqu'à cet été que notre groupe avait détenu de 1961 à 1991 un immeuble construit sur des terrains dont l'un avait été la propriété de vos parents. Une spoliation constitue une atteinte intolérable aux droits de la personne humaine et doit certainement être réparée. Je suis personnellement attaché à ce que le groupe que je préside soit irréprochable. Dans le même temps, le mandat dont je suis investi m'interdit d'utiliser les fonds sociaux sans fondement et vous comprendrez certainement que je ne puisse envisager le paiement d'une somme de plus de 200 millions de francs au vu d'une réclamation dont tous les éléments n'auraient pas été préalablement vérifiés.

L'extrême complexité de la situation résultant de l'ancienneté des faits, de leur déroulement en Allemagne, de ce que trois propriétaires se sont succédés depuis la vente de 1938, de l'intervention passée d'une juridiction allemande statuant en droit allemand dont les règles me paraissent devoir continuer à s'appliquer, m'interdit encore de formuler une opinion définitive.

Pour me permettre d'apprécier votre demande, des vérifications et des consultations s'imposent. Il me semble notamment que les dossiers et les explications que pourraient fournir la compagnie d'assurance allemande, dont je présume qu'elle est également et en premier lieu votre interlocutrice puisqu'elle a détenu l'immeuble de 1938 à 1954, devraient permettre de mieux comprendre la situation.

Je ne voudrais pas que vous imaginiez que mon attitude est dictée par une volonté dilatoire, c'est pourquoi, c'est bien volontiers que je vous propose de participer aux frais que pourraient entraîner pour vous en Allemagne les recherches et les consultations nécessaires à l'instruction du dossier.

Si vous acceptez cette proposition qui a pour objet de vous aider dans votre recherche de la vérité, ce que je souhaite de tout cœur, vous voudrez bien me le faire savoir, soit directement, soit par l'intermédiaire de nos avocats respectifs qui auront pour mission d'en faciliter la mise en œuvre.

Je vous prie d'agréer, Madame, l'expression de mes sentiments distingués.

Lindsay OWEN-JONES

Translation

L'ORÉAL

Clichy, 4 October 2001

Madame Edith Waitzfelder

c/Me Charles Korman
66,avenue Kléber
75116–Paris

c/Madame Monica Waitzfelder
2, place Charles Bernard
75018–Paris

Madame,

Maître Charles Korman wrote to me in your name on 18 June in order to draw my attention to your situation and ask me to pay you on behalf of the group I head a total of 60,556,726 DM in order to compensate you for the robbery your parents were victims of as a result of the Nazi regime.

As you know, I asked our lawyers to contact yours in order to become acquainted with the case and be well informed thereon.

I understand that the actions that give rise to this affair concern the purchase in 1938 by a German insurance company of a building situate in Karlsruhe in Germany and belonging to your parents who were German citizens at the time. In 1951 a Jewish association, legally appointed to take the place of the Jews exterminated by the Nazi regime, and your uncle, a survivor from the Shoah, whose heir you are, legally challenged this acquisition and then signed an agreement with the insurance company which was endorsed by the German judge for Restitutions, a special judicial process put in place by the Allies after the war.

In 1954, the L'Oréal subsidiary <u>in Germany, in which the group bought back shares only in 1961</u>, acquired the land which included the buildings destroyed by bombing raids. This land was incorporated into a larger complex, and resold in 1991.

I have learned of this situation on reading the letter from your lawyer and I was unaware until this summer that <u>our group had owned from 1961 to 1991 a building</u> constructed on plots one of which had been your parents' property. A theft constitutes an intolerable attack on the rights of human beings and must certainly be redressed. I am personally committed to the group that I head being above reproach. At the same time, the mandate with which I am charged prevents me from using social funds without proper reason and you will certainly understand that I cannot envisage the payment of a sum of more than 200 million francs on sight of a claim in which every element has not been previously checked.

The extreme complexity of the situation resulting from the past nature of these acts, from their taking place in Germany, from the fact that there have been three owners since the sale in 1938, from the intervention made under German jurisdiction based on German law the rules of which I think must still continue to apply, prevent me from reaching a definitive conclusion.

In order to be able to consider your request, I need to check and consult. I believe in particular that the files and explanations that could be supplied by the German insurance company with which I assume you are also and primarily in contact since it owned the building from 1938 to 1954, should allow us a clearer understanding of the situation.

I would not want you to imagine my attitude is dictated by a desire to delay matters, that is why I am very happy to contribute towards the expenses you might accrue in Germany in your researches and consultations necessary for the preparation of your dossier.

If you accept this offer the aim of which is to help you in your search for the truth, which I sincerely desire, would you be so kind to let me know, either directly, or through the mediation of our respective lawyers who will be charged with putting this in place.

Yours sincerely,

Lindsay OWEN-JONES

12

BGV Internal Memorandum

BGV.   Karlsruhe, den 4.Juni 1951.

I. Aktenvermerk: Betr.: Hausgrundstück Wendtstr. 19.

Am 2.6.1951 teilte Herr Rechtsanwalt Dr. Sickinger fernmündlich mit, dass Herr Dr. Karl Rosenfelder z. Zt. in Deutschland weile u. ihm beauftragt habe, seinen Rückerstattungsanspruch aus dem Hausbesitz Wendtstr. 19 gegen uns zu verfolgen. Er erkundigte sich nach dem Stand der Angelegenheit und ich gab ihm Auskunft über die Ablehnung der IRSO. Herr Dr.Sickinger wird veranlassen, dass Herr Dr.Karl Rosenfelder sich umgehend mit der IRSO in Verbindung setzt um zu erreichen, dass diese die Angelegenheit an ihn abgibt. Dann soll gemeinsam die Frage geprüft werden, ob eine vergleichsweise Erledigung angebracht und möglich ist. Sollte es nicht zu einem Vergleich kommen, wird Herr Rechtsanwalt Dr.Sickinger das Mandat gegen uns niederlegen, da er nicht gegen uns auftreten will.

II. Z.d.A.

Translation

BGV.

1. Memorandum for file

Subject: land built on Wendtstr.19

On 02/06/1951, Mr Sickinger, lawyer, informed me by telephone that Dr Karl Rosenfelder presently resided in Germany and that he had charged him with establishing, against us, his right for restitution in relation to the property situate Wendstr, 19. He enquired how advanced this matter was, and I informed him of the rejection on the part of the JRSO. Mr Sickinger will make sure that Dr. Karl Rosenfelder gets into contact as soon as possible with the JRSO so that the latter can deal with the matter. <u>Then it will be necessary to examine the whole business to decide if the settling of this issue by negotiation is opportune and possible. If an agreement proves impossible, Mr Sickinger will renounce his brief, for he has no wish to intervene against us.</u>

II. attached to file

13

Letter Signed by *Maître* Sickinger, Dating from September 1934 and Bearing the Swastika

Bund National-Sozialiſtiſcher Deutſcher Juriſten

Gau Baden ✦ Landesgerichtsbezirk Karlsruhe

Bezirksfachgruppe
Rechtsanwälte Karlsruhe.

S/He.

Anſchrift
Bezirksfachgruppenleiter
Rechtsanwalt Dr. Sickinger
Karlsruhe, Kaiſerſtr. 199

Karlsruhe, den 11. September 34

An den

Vorstand der Badischen Anwaltskammer

Herrn Rechtsanwalt Brombacher

K a r l s r u h e .

, nimmt aber neue nur auf

seinen eigenen Namen an .

Gegen das Verhalten von Dr. Krämer dürften hiernach
Bedenken nicht bestehen .

Mit kolleg. Hochachtung

Rechtsanwalt .

14

Affidavit Made by Process-Server on 19 September 2001 on the Content of the L'Oréal Internet Site

3

Elle propose l'arborescence suivante : "l'OREAL DEUTSCHLAND".

Je clique sur ce lien et j'arrive sur une page contenant la mention « PORTRÄT », que j'imprime sur deux pages et constituant l'**annexe 2**. Cette page d'accueil comporte un menu vertical, faisant apparaître les rubriques suivantes :

- GRUSSWORT
- ZAHLEN UND FAKTEN
- GESCHICHTE
- UMWELT
- QUALITATSSICHERUNG

Je clique sur la rubrique "GESCHICHTE" et apparaît à l'écran une page intitulée " GESCHICHTE " que j'imprime pour constituer l'**Annexe 3**.

Je reproduis littéralement le premier paragraphe de cette page :

« Den Grundstein dieser einzigartigen Erfolgsgeschichte legt André Tondu 1930 in Berlin, als er von dem französischen Firmengründer Eugène Schueller beauftragt wird, den deutschen Friseurmarkt zu erobern. Dabei sind die Anfänge der Haarfarben und Parfümerien GmbH (HUP) nicht leicht. Zwar finden die ersten Colorationen schnell Anklang, doch das Berliner Werk wird im Krieg zerstört, und 1945 muß in Karlsruhe eine neue Fabrik gebaut werden. »

Je me connecte ensuite sur le site Internet http://www.atendo.de

Une page de présentation du site apparaît que j'imprime et constituant l'**annexe 4**.

Société Civile Professionnelle
**Maurice ESKENAZI ~ André HADJEDJ
Et Didier BENHAMOU**
Huissiers de Justice associés
2, Rue de la Roquette
75011 PARIS
☎ 01 49 23 81 00

Translation

She suggests the following connection: 'L'ORÉAL DEUTSCHLAND'

I click on the link and reach a page containing the mention 'PORTRÄT', that I print out on two pages and that constitutes Appendix 2. This welcome page carries a vertical menu, where the following headings appear:

GRUSSWORT
ZAHLEN UND FAKTEN
GESCHICHTE
UMWELT
QUALITATSSICHERUNG

I click on the 'GESCHICHTE' heading, and a page entitled 'GESCHICHTE' appears on the screen that I print out and which constitutes Appendix 3.

I reproduce literally the first paragraph from this page:

'The foundation stone of this unparalleled success was laid in 1930 in Berlin by André TONDU, when Eugène Schueller the founder of the French firm charges him with conquest of the German hairdressing market. The beginnings of Haarfarben und Parfümerien GmbH (HUP) are not easy. Certainly, the first dyes are quickly accepted by the market, but the base in Berlin was destroyed during the war, and in 1945, a new factory will be built in Karlsruhe.'

I then went to the Internet site http://www.atendo.de

I print out the page introducing the site and it constitutes Appendix 4

Société Civile Professionnelle
Maurice ESKENAZI – ANDRÉ HADJEDJ
Et Didier BENHAMOU
Huissiers de justice associés
2, Rue de la Roquette
75011 PARIS
TEL 01 49 23 81 00

15

Extract from the Magazine of the L'Oréal Joint Production
Committee Dated November 1948

La HAARFARBEN, d'abord à BERLIN, maintenant à KARLSRUHE, avec son manager de toujours, M. Tondu, l'OREAL-HOLLAND, l'A-B-OREAL-SUEDE à STOCKHOLM où Marcel Stein s'est installé, l'OREAL-CANADA.

En Afrique du Nord, la Société AZURVILLE à ALGER et l'U.F.C.I. à CASABLANCA pour laquelle M. Raymond a quitté Pantin.

Et dans tous les pays du monde, les agences OREAL sont installées et travaillent : en AFRIQUE DU SUD, en ANGLETERRE, en AUTRICHE, en AUSTRALIE, en BULGARIE, au CHILI, en COLOMBIE et à CUBA, en EGYPTE, en PALESTINE, au PEROU, au PORTUGAL, en URUGUAY.

Partout l'OREAL, encore l'OREAL, toujours l'OREAL...

Translation

The HAARFARBEN, first in BERLIN, now in KARLSRUHE, managed as always by Mr Tondu, L'OREAL-HOLLAND, L'A-B-OREAL-SWEDEN in STOCKHOLM where Marcel Stein is in place, L'OREAL-CANADA.

In North Africa, the AZURVILLE Company and the U.F.C.I. in CASABLANCA for which Mr RAYMOND left Pantin.

And branches of L'OREAL have been set up and are working in all the countries of the world: in SOUTH AFRICA, in ENGLAND, in AUSTRIA, in AUSTRALIA, in BULGARIA, in CHILE, in COLOMBIA and CUBA, in EGYPT, in PALESTINE, in PERU, in PORTUGAL, in URUGUAY.

L'OREAL everywhere, L'OREAL for ever, L'OREAL for always...

16

Extracts from the Magazine of the L'Oréal Joint Production Committee Dated March 1949

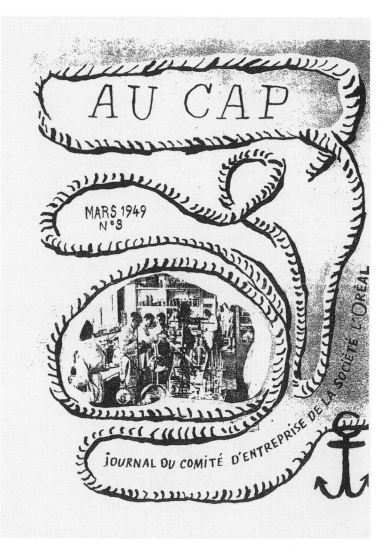

Le 11 décembre 1948 avait lieu la fête de fin d'année de la HAARFARBEN UND PARFUMERIE à KARLSRUHE.

Nous devons à la gentillesse de M. TONDU, notre ami de toujours, d'avoir les textes qui ont été écrits par le personnel à l'occasion de cette manifestation.

M. ZORAYAN, de l'usine de La Courneuve a bien voulu nous en faire la traduction et nous l'en remercions.

La place nous manquant pour reproduire tous les textes, nous avons reproduit les différentes maquettes qui illustraient ces textes.

Hommage rendu à l'OREAL pour ses fabrications, l'ouverture disait en substance :

La devise de la firme reste toujours :
« Le meilleur pour la femme. »

Après une évocation de la teinture, en faisant spirituellement appel à la sagesse... animal', les tableaux défilaient tour à tour sur la Chimie, la Physique, la Science, la Technique oratoire, l'Astronomie.

L'affirmation finale rejoignait la première :

IMEDIA teint toujours merveilleusement :
Toutes nuances pour tous cheveux.

Et nous citons le chant de la firme qui n'a. malheureusement pas la même saveur dans la traduction :

Dans tous les pays et dans toutes les régions,
Partout où les hommes habitent, en entend
La mère dire à son enfant,
Le père à son fils avec enthousiasme,
Dans tout le monde, enfin, un seul écho :
« Tous, nous n'utilisons que l'OREAL ».

Bravo, M. TONDU et merci d'avoir bien voulu faire cette liaison KARLSRUHE PARIS.

Translation

On 11 December 1948 the HAARFARBEN UND PARFUMERIE in Karlsruhe held its end of the year party.

We give thanks to the kind Mr Tondu, our friend as always, for sending the texts written by staff on the occasion of this event.

Mr ZORAYAN, from the factory in La Courneuve translated them for us, and we thank him for that.

Since we don't have the space to reproduce all the texts we reproduce the different designs that illustrate these texts.

Homage is paid to L'Oréal for its products, the opening says in substance:
> The motto of our firm remains as always:
> 'The best women can have'

After evoking their dyes, and making a spiritual appeal to animal…wisdom, the scenes parade by in focus on Chemistry, Physics, Oratory technique, Astronomy.

The final statement returns to the first:
> IMEDIA always dyes wonderfully:
> Every shade for every hair.

And we will quote the company song that unfortunately doesn't have the same flavour in translation:
> In every country and in every region,
> Everywhere where men dwell, we hear
> Mothers their children tell,
> Fathers their sons excitedly,
> Throughout the world, in a single echo:
> 'We all use only l'OREAL'

Bravo, Mr Tondu and thank you for wanting to make this KARLSRUHE–PARIS link.

Tract from the MSR Executive Committee

REFAIRE LA FRANCE

Chef : EUGENE DELONCLE.

Chef adjoint et remplaçant du Chef :
JEAN FONTENOY.

Comité executif (réunissant les chefs des grands services, conseillers techniques pour l'exécution des ordres du Chef et du Chef adjoint).

Président et dirigeant de toutes les Commissions techniques et Comités d'études .. SCHUELLER.

Service de renseignements .. FILLIOL

Région parisienne .... { CORREZE (à la Légion)
{ CHARBONNEAU

Organisation territoriale .... FAURAN

C. E. R. F. A. T. .... SOULES

Propagande, Presse .... CHRISTOPHE

Pour tout ce qui concerne le Secrétariat général, s'adresser, provisoirement, sous cette rubrique, au 80, rue Saint-Lazare.

Des précisions seront fournies à nos amis et aux sections dès la semaine prochaine.

Comité exécutif du M.S.R. ████████████████████████████

Translation

REMAKING FRANCE

Head: EUGENE DELONCLE.
Joint head and deputy head: JEAN FONTENOY

Executive committee (including heads of main services, technical advisers for the carrying out of the head and joint heads' orders).
Chair and leader of all
Technical Commissions
and Research Committees.... SCHUELLER
Information service.......... FILLIOL
Paris Region...............{ CORREZE (At the Legion)
                            CHARBONNEAU
Territorial organization....... FAURAN
C.E.R.F.A.T................ SOULES
Publicity, Press............. CHRISTOPHE

For anything concerning General administrative business, provisionally write, under this rubric, to 80, rue Saint-Lazare.
More details will be supplied to our friends and sections next week.

Executive Committee of the M.S.R.

Newspaper Cutting Mentioning Eugène Schueller, Chairman of the MSR Technical Committee, the Secretariat of Which was Based at 14 rue Royale

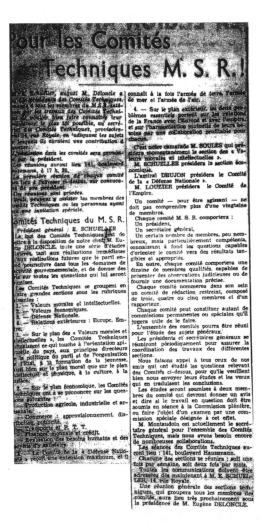

Translation

For the M.S.R. Technical Committees!

Mr E. Schueller, to whom Mr Deloncle has entrusted the chairmanship of the Technical Committees asks all M.S.R. members involved in the work of the Technical Committees to communicate as soon as possible their candidacy, to the secretary of the Technical Committees, provisionally at 14 rue Royale, indicating the subjects on which they would like to make a contribution.

Membership of the committees will be decided by the chair.

Meetings will take place at 141 boulevard Haussmann, at 17.30.

The first meeting of each committee will take place at the above address, convened by the chair.

These meetings are private.

Only members of the Technical Committees or specially invited people may attend.

Technical Committees of the M.S.R.

General chair: E. SCHUELLER

The aim of the Technical Committees is to put at the disposition of our head Mr Eugène DELONCLE a whole series of studies related as much to immediate as to future endeavours that the party will pursue in every domain of government activity, and to give help on all issues it faces.

The Technical Committees are grouped in four important sections under the following headings:

1 – Moral and intellectual values.

2 – Economic values.

3 – National Defence.

4 – Foreign relations: Europe, Empire.

1 – In the area of 'Moral and intellectual values', the Technical Committees will define what concerns the spiritual orientation of the country, the main lines of the policies of the party and the organization of the State, the training of the youth, morally, intellectually and physically, culture and justice.

2 – In the area of economics the Technical Committees must give a lead on the following questions:

Agricultural, industrial and craft production.

Trade, supplies, distribution, advertising.

Transport and Telecommunications.

Finance, money and credit.

Evaluation of human needs and ways of satisfying them.

3. – The Committee for National Defence is all encompassing and includes the army, air force and navy.

4 – On external issues, the two main areas concern France's relations with Europe and with the Empire and the mutual harmonization of their needs for a collaboration that will be profitable for each party.

It is our comrade Mr SOULES who will for the moment chair the section for 'Moral and intellectual values'.

Mr SCHUELLER will chair the economics section.

Admiral DRUJON will chair the committee for 'National Defence'.

Mr LOUZIER will chair the Committee for the Empire.

A committee – in order to function – must not comprise more than twenty members.

Each M.S.R. committee will comprise:

A chair

A general secretary

A few members – not too many – but who are particularly competent to understand the relevant issues and able to direct the committee to tangible, appropriate results.

Moreover, each committee will have ten qualified members able to provide judicious opinions or necessary documentation.

Each committee will appoint a small editorial committee comprising three, four or five members and a rapporteur.

Each committee can constitute as many permanent or special commissions as it thinks useful.

All committees can be brought together to study general issues.

Chairs and general secretaries will meet regularly to ensure the coordination of the work of the different sections.

We appeal to all those of our friends who have studied the relevant issues for the above mentioned committees, to send us their analyses and the conclusions that arise from them.

The studies will be submitted to two members of the committee who will give an opinion and say whether the study in question should be put before a plenary session or should be the object of an examination by a special commission designated to that end.

Mr Montaudoin is currently the general secretary for all the Technical Committees, but we need many other collaborators.

The Technical Committees will meet at 141, boulevard Haussmann,

Each of the sections will meet once a week, that is twice a month.

All communications must be addressed from now on to Mr E.SCHUELLER, 14 rue Royale.

A general meeting of the technical committees bringing together all the members of the committees will take place shortly under the chairmanship of Mr Eugène DELONCLE.

Acknowledgements

Monique Queirel; Évelyne Queirel; Paulette Queirel; Anne Schuchman; Domique Missika; Sylvie Vormus; *maître* Charles Korman; *maître* Charles Choucroy; *maître* Charles Morel; *maître* Bernard Jouaneau; Christian Poslaniec; Jean-Marc Heller; Angela Kohler; Jérémy Fiedler; Bernard Monge; Diane Kuperman; François Giustiniani; Aude Gillon; Jean-Pierre Pelletier; Jean Frydman; the World Jewish Congress; *maître* Serge Klarsfeld; Beate Klarsfeld; the Centre for Contemporary Jewish Documentation; Nicole Yardeni; Bruno Abescat; Diane Kamienny; Jean-Marc Dreyfus; Karine Vidal; Thal Bruttmann; Vincent Frank; Alexandre Garcia; the editorial board of *Le Monde*; the research department of L'Opéra-Bastille; the research department of the Théâtre du Châtelet; Charles Ageorge; Carlos Proenza; Sylvie Dubois; Pierrette Chastel; Tino Müller; Csaba Airizer; Frau Fetzner; Dr Koch; Philippe Sprang; Alexandre Ifi; Mathias Widmaier; Didier Benoit; Helio Limoeiro; Camille Bonamy; Amanda Dalton; Mme V.; Jean Kahn, President of the Central Consistory Court; Dominique Verdeilhan; Philippe Délerac; Marie-Amélie Lombard; Martine Archambault; Agnès Gardet; Jean-Philippe Deniou; Nicolas Marut; Michel Zerbib; Sebastien Laugenie; André Darmon; Eugène Leiba; Joelle Perelberg; Arielle Lellouch; Laurent Léger; Helène Keller Lind; Laurent Valdiguié; Niels Klawitter; Sue Hoppough; Sarah Wildman; Amelia Gentleman; Jack Gee; Commission Culture B; BBF; Gérard Ulmo; Charles Leselbaum; Arno Klarsfeld; Michel Chetrit; Joseph Hattab; Loge Ben Gurion; Thierry Lascard; Rodolph Cahn; Yaël König; Ilan Katz; Robert Bader; Martinianne; Wizo; Monik Kern; Laurent Kern; Pierre Levy; Barbara Lèfebvre; Cécilia Gabiizon; B'nai Brith France.

I would equally like to thank all the friends who have given me such support.